Looking

for

the

Other

Side

Looking for the Other Side

SHERRY SUIB COHEN

FOREWORD BY DEEPAK CHOPRA

The extraordinary adventures of a skeptical journalist as she explores the non-material world, visiting psychics, mediums, astrologers, tarot readers, an oracle, a channeler, parapsychologists, a tea leaf reader, a numerologist, a past-life regressor, and a dowser—searching for her mom, herself, and why we're here.

CLARKSON POTTER / PUBLISHERS   NEW YORK

Published by Clarkson Potter/Publishers, 201 East 50th Street, New York, New York 10022. Member of the Crown Publishing Group.

Random House, Inc. New York, Toronto, London, Sydney, Auckland

http://www.randomhouse.com/

Clarkson N. Potter, Potter, and colophon are trademarks of Clarkson N. Potter, Inc.

Printed in the United States of America

Library of Congress Cataloging-in-Publication Data

Cohen, Sherry Suib.
    Looking for the other side/
Sherry Suib Cohen.
        p.   cm.
    Includes bibliographical references.
        1. Parapsychology.   2. Occultism.   3. Cohen, Sherry Suib.
    I. Title.
    BF1031.C587   1996
    133—dc20   96-29191
                        CIP

ISBN 0-517-70828-0

10   9   8   7   6   5   4   3   2   1

First Edition

For blue-eyed Julia Iren.
I wish her many worlds and
an open mind.

Contents

Acknowledgments

NONE OF IT WOULD HAVE HAPPENED WITHOUT *New Woman* magazine. This book was born in its pages. The magazine strives always to stretch the imagination of its readers, and it does as much for its writers. Senior editor Stephanie von Hirschberg, executive editor Susan Kane, and editor in chief Betsy Carter have reconstituted my thinking and sent me on extraordinary journeys: I cannot thank them enough, these terrific women, these funny, wise friends. My deep gratitude also to Jeannette Benny, director of *New Woman's* editorial services, who was the gatekeeper for the myriad letters from readers when my article "Looking for Mom" first appeared. I'm immensely privileged to be part of *New Woman,* I can't wait to see what they next come up with for me, and I hope they never throw me out.

My brilliant editor, Carol Southern, a true believer in this book, really knows what's *out there* and has taught me: she's a visionary mentor with impeccable judgment.

Thanks, of course, to my powerhouse agent, Connie Clausen, who has given me the career of my dreams, who asks more of me than I ever imagined I owned, and worse, who makes me deliver! She's my life friend. And to Lisa Kaiser and Stedman Mays at the Clausen agency, whose inspiration and terrific tips were wonderful.

Thanks also to Eliza Scott at Clarkson Potter, who has held my hand through two books now: she has a warm, empowering grasp.

My gratitude as well for their generous suggestions to John Harber, David Margulies, Maggie Blackman, Gloria DiGennaro, Angelika Weller, Susan Freeman, Joanna McMann, David Cahn, Ellen Stoianoff, Nancy Clark, Nancymarie Jones, Lois Cogen, and Barbara Appel; to Jan Goodwin, at whose home I first started opening my mind; to Larry Ashmead, who kept me laughing and reading throughout the long, testy opening of that mind; to the 92 Street Y Aisle, which daily lends its naked support, especially Eleanor Donnenfeld, Carol Tannenhauser, Susan Scopetta, Susan Schermer, Betsy Jablow, Jill Newhouse, Lisa Hsia, and Marcy Miller; and to the Group—Marjorie Austrian, Sybil Evans, Teri Seidman, who are my childhood roots and my grown-up oaks.

As always, my grateful love to my children, Susan Gross and Adam Cohen, Jennifer and Steven Goldstein—and to Becky, Josh, and Julia: their collected beauty is dazzling.

Surely the memory of my darling, intricate, vivid mother, Jane, will always inspire me. And to David, my dad—and to Audrey Plummer: I love you.

To Larry Cohen: No man like this one ever lived.

Penetrating so many secrets,
we cease to believe in the
unknowable.
But there it sits,
nevertheless, calmly licking
its chops.

H. L. MENCKEN

Foreword

IT IS A TRIBUTE TO THE EMERGING MATURITY of our civilization that our world is coming to grips with the reality of spirit as a real force. This mysterious force, curving back within itself, expresses itself as form and phenomenon. Sherry Suib Cohen's book gives you a glimpse of a world that lies beyond the illusion of appearance. This deeper reality exists beyond our senses and connects us with patterns of intelligence that permeate the whole cosmos. I congratulate Sherry Suib Cohen for being a pioneer/explorer of this world, which science is only just beginning to glimpse.

When Cohen, as a skeptical journalist, decided to allow herself to be open to energies outside her long-held beliefs, she began a journey that would bring her a panoply of lyrical, comic, insightful, and inspirational experiences. As she got beyond the limitations of her own ego judgments about what *should happen*—she found a world of *what is.*

Intellectually, Cohen held to the belief that she was, first and foremost, a physical being. Exploring the world of spirit she gradually began to see that first and foremost, she was a *subtle* being who could create new selves and rediscover past selves on countless levels, seen and unseen. She found that reaching into unseen worlds doesn't make one feel foolish, after all: instead, it allows one to marshall all the intelligence of the universe, compressing billions of years of knowledge into every second of present life. It allows one to connect in layers and through layers to a universal experience. Trusting in the universe enabled Sherry to become a body in a soul rather than a soul in a body.

Looking for the Other Side jogs the reader into refining awareness and going, with the author, beyond the five senses into unimaginable realms. As Sherry Suib Cohen learned not to scoff at other possibilities and other energies, she came to throw off fear and realize the pure spirit within. No journey could be more wondrous.

DEEPAK CHOPRA, M.D.

Part I | Looking for Mom

> One does not become
> enlightened by imagining
> figures of light, but by making
> the darkness conscious.
> CARL JUNG

> Few men have imagination
> enough for reality.
> JOHANN WOLFGANG
> VON GOETHE

Skeptic in a Strange Land

IF YOU'RE GOING TO READ THIS BOOK, I want to tell you a little about me.

I'm a journalist. I'm a skeptic. I challenge everything. I look up things in the library, a lot. I need proof, proof, proof. Although in the scary moments I find myself praying to God (hey, you never know), I am constitutionally doubtful about Him or even Her, astrology, psychics, channeling, reincarnation, and tarot. I don't even want to *hear* about past-life regression. At least, it was that way.

Two years ago my mother died. I'm an only child, and we had a powerful relationship, loving but complicated. She was wise, lioness-protective, killingly critical. The death of a parent threatens our own lives. It proves we're mortal, that our days are limited, that life is temporal, not eternal. Life is a disappearing act, and my mother disappeared on me.

I couldn't believe she was really gone. We had a lot of unfinished business between us, and was it possible I was never again going to grit my teeth and hear her tell me, "Wear your pearls"?

A year after her death I was having a girls' night out with four of the most intelligent women I knew. One was a journalist for *The New York Times*. Another had nursed lepers with Mother Theresa, traded barbs with Margaret Thatcher, and spent time escaping helicopter gunfire as she traveled with Afghan freedom fighters. Another was a *Ladies Home Journal* editor and the last, my own editor from *New Woman* magazine. I was psyched for gossip, networking, eating. Halfway through drinks it appeared we were soon to be six. One of us had invited her astrologer friend to come. My heart sank.

When the astrologer arrived, just as I suspected, the tenor of the evening changed: the talk was of reading the stars, psychic phenomena, paranormal experiences. I couldn't bear it. How was it possible that these brave, smart women shared mediums and psychics, shared tarot readers and numerologists, shared everything except my dubious, critical journalist's heart? What was it about their life paths that had them hooked on trying to communicate with the dead, reading the planets, visiting a faith healer instead of a trusty orthopedist?

All evening we spoke of things mystical. I felt faintly disgusted and very disappointed. I thought they were naive.

They thought I was arrogant and closed-minded: they made no bones about telling me that. They all pretty much thought that judging matters of which one had no personal knowledge was the height of cynicism.

Stephanie von Hirschberg, my *New Woman* editor, took things into her own hands. She knew of my mother's recent death and assigned me a story right then and there. "Look for your mom, Sherry," she said. "See for yourself if there's more to people than flesh and bone. Visit mediums. Lose that ironclad shell—try to be objective. See if any of your mom is left, if she resides on some other plane out there, just out of reach—or maybe even within reach. . . ."

Secretly I'd always wanted to try something like this—much in the same way I would have liked to try ballooning. It seemed so trendy, though, and I'd have felt like a jerk. So I never did.

But now I had an assignment. That shed a different light on

everything. Now I could go as a reporter, dispassionate, critical, always hiding behind a tape recorder. I wouldn't have to get really involved.

Also, I had to admit that I wanted my mom back, if only for a moment, wanted to know if she was frightened when she died, wanted some last minute instructions from her. If there was the remotest chance . . .

And that was the genesis for this book. It started with looking for Mom, and like Topsy, it grew.

It changed my life.

This is the story of what happened to me.

The Mediums

There are more things in heaven and earth, Horatio,
Than are dreamt of in your philosophy.

                                                    HAMLET

LILY DALE

IT'S TIME TO BEGIN MY JOURNEY, time to go out on the road
looking for Mom via the medium of mediums. Everything I've
ever learned tells me I'm a fool to even try, but if there's even a
hope of a hope—listen Mom, I'm on my way. You always said I
was stubborn: if you're there, I'll find you.

My first break comes when I spot an article in an unlikely place—
the very formal and conservative *Wall Street Journal:* it's about a tiny
town called Lily Dale where mediums really are the message. The
167-acre Spiritualist compound of two hundred pretty little ginger-
bready Victorian houses in a dreamy, pastoral setting sits on the
banks of peaceful Cassadaga Lake. The town is supported by devo-
tees of the Spiritualist Church—Christians who believe that the human soul survives death and is able to connect with the living
through intermediaries. I'm on my way to Lily Dale, musing about
what to expect, and the toll bridge collector sets the stage.

"How far to Lily Dale?" I ask.

"Stay on this road," he answers, "left at the light, eight miles
down to Cassadaga, and then follow the vibes."

Oh, God, I think.

From early June through Labor Day visiting and resident mediums commune with believers who want to contact loved ones in "spirit." Thirty-three thousand corporeal visitors descended on Lily Dale in the summer of 1995, and who knows how many of the other kind stopped by.

The people I see today are young and old, dressed in suits but also jeans, quiet and chattering—and what they have in common is that no one's kidding around. These are earnest people desperate to speak with lost children, fathers, aunts, wives.

My private reading with medium Betty Marlowe (this is not her real name) has been scheduled for late in the afternoon, so I have time. I let myself be swept along by the other seekers to Inspiration Stump in Leolyn Woods, a jade virgin forest of looming beeches and maples, for a communal fresh air service.

Sunlight dapples a circle where rows of benches are set up in front of a huge wooden tree stump. Towering trees whisper. The effect is that of an exalted outdoor cathedral, touched with a scent of pine.

Who's here, waiting for—*something*—at Inspiration Stump?

An older man with a leg brace.

A guy in black leather motorcycle duds, Harley-Davidson boots, one silver cross dangling from his right ear, and a million keys competing with a million chains.

A beautiful girl in a wheelchair equipped with an oxygen tank, which she wears. Oxygen!

A gnarled woman who says she's been coming here for fifty-eight years.

Someone who looks like me.

A kindly-sounding man stands, asks us to join him in a prayer, and then introduces the first visiting medium, curly-haired Patricia from Texas, who stands in front of the stump and searches the audience as if she's looking for a particular person.

"You—in the white blouse," she calls to a young woman. "Spirit says he wants to talk to you. He's wrapping his arms around you, he looks elderly, a grandfather, maybe?"

The young woman nods violently.

"Speak up—I need to hear your voice," the medium admonishes her. "Yes, thank you. Spirit says he sees a change happening for you soon, something about books, you're not finished with your education yet—and there's something about a sixteen-month-old baby in your life—does that make sense to you?"

The woman looks puzzled.

"Well, it *will*," says Patricia the medium. "And Spirit says he sees a brand-new wedding band on your finger."

The man sitting beside the woman, obviously her husband, looks startled. Nervous laughter floods the clearing. "Listen, I don't think Spirit's saying you're going to have another husband," consoles the medium, "just maybe a brand-new wedding band."

"I hear a Bob—a Robert being called," continues the medium, her eyes closed. "Is there a Robert here?"

What a surprise. There is. An older man calls out with delight.

"Well, there's a Jane looking for you."

I feel a sudden sharp anguish. My mother is Jane. Maybe the medium got us mixed up and it's me Jane wants.

But no, Robert thinks about it and he also seems to know a departed Jane.

"Spirit says you take on more than you can handle," reports the medium. The man nods ruefully. "Your legs hurt, especially the left one."

Robert's hand goes down to rub his left leg.

"And, there's a tiny woman here with white hair and she's shoving a loaf of bread in the oven and she wants you to know she's well—does that make any sense?"

The man is incredulous. "My mother," he can barely whisper.

"And," the medium goes on, "she's feeding you white tea—hot water with milk and sugar, do you remember?"

He tries, but no, he doesn't.

"Don't feel guilty," the medium *consoles* (???), "just because you don't remember. But, *that's white tea I see.*"

The man concedes the possibility.

Four more mediums take turns. Sometimes they hit, sometimes they miss, and always they cover the miss with generalities. I love the forest, but I don't believe a word of it. And my mother's not here.

BETTY MARLOWE

Medium Betty Marlowe's house has a lot of figures on the front lawn—a dwarf, a Bambi, a kitten, and a swan. She also has an enormous television antenna: I hope it gives her greater access.

I'm wearing my mother's worn wedding ring (how tiny it is—I never realized her fingers were so thin!) on a chain around my neck, her navy felt skirt that still carries a few of her gray hairs in its crevices, and The Pearls. I hope it brings us close.

I tell Betty that I'm a journalist doing a story on looking for my mom because I don't want to be there under false pretenses, and she tells me at the outset, "You know, you just can't summon up the dead, you have to wait and see who comes, but I think we may just get lucky, and listen—this is my religion, don't whack it up in your story."

Betty's wearing black sweat pants and a necromancer's gold sunburst on a black sweatshirt. Large triangular glasses cloak crinkly eyes. She's about seventy, and she has a nice way as she sits opposite me in a small parlor.

"Take a deep breath," she instructs. Then she's off and running, a mile a minute this woman speaks. There's a half hour of the following:

"We'll be dealing with health, wealth, self, and self-image. I'm picking up a gentleman who left with a heart condition, no?"

No.

"I'm dealing with another in spirit—this is just wonderful, wonderful—another who left with cancer. She's got lots of spunk and fuchsia around her, and she's sending out a lot of warmth and energy to you. Yes?"

No.

"Well, here's a younger person who went very tragically, a car accident, no? A bicycle, no?"

No.

"Well, was your mother one of those people who gave continuously, she gave and gave to you? I want to go with cooking . . . did she cook? I see her baking breads. . . . There's lots of pinks and energy here, she sends you peace and stability, says you're going to the Southwest soon, says you will get a new computer soon, says you like deadlines. I see lots of color and music from the spirit world. Spirit says, 'We have symphony here, too, what did you think?' Spirit says to slow down, says you're to eat your veggies and drink your juices, says you're going to buy new shoes soon. You know, Sherry, your mom's a young spirit, it usually takes five to ten years to make contact, we got lucky."

No, we didn't.

I don't want to whack her religion, but my mother's not there. Back at the Maplewood Hotel in Lily Dale, the sign in the worn lobby says "Please, No Readings, Séances or Healings in the Hotel Lobby."

Mediumship

Who would believe it? At Harvard last year, more than one-quarter of the freshman class expressed an interest in "after-death" studies. Call it postlife chic, call it putting a positive spin on death—why the sudden popularity of mediumship?

Naturally I begin my research at the libraries: it's safe there. I want to find out, for starters, who believes in mediumship and in the paranormal in general. More people than you'd dream. At the American Society for Psychical Research, I discover a 1990 Gallup poll showing that Americans expressed a belief in the existence of paranormal, ghostly, and otherwordly experiences to an astonishing degree. One in six Americans feel they've been in touch with someone who's died—and often this happens through the intervention of a medium. Nearly half of all Americans believe there is such a thing as psychic or spiritual healing. Only 7 percent of Americans denied believing in any of a list of eighteen paranormal experiences presented by Gallup, a list that includes a belief in mediums, telepathy, and horoscopes. But how many reputable mediums live in this country? I want to find some proof of reliability.

Zero luck, zilch, nothing. On the issue of mediums I discover no serious, controlled studies, no authenticated data. There's an explanation for that, and I hear it at the library of the Parapsychology Foundation: the reason I've been having so much trouble finding data on mediums, says spokesperson Joanna McMann, Ph.D., is that there is no acceptable criteria for studying life after death. In fact, says Dr. McMann, any scam artist can say she's a medium. There's no accredited test one has to pass, no association that rules on the competence of those who call themselves mediums, sensitives, or psychics. To be fair, anyone also can put out a shingle advertising herself as a psychotherapist, without benefit of test or license.

Mediumship is an ancient and universal practice; there have even been stories of mediums in the Bible—the account, for example, of the Witch of Endor, who had a "familiar spirit" and who, at King Saul's request, conjured up the ghost of Samuel.

Modern American mediumship can be traced to the activities in 1848 of the not-so-shy medium Margaret Fox and her sisters who eventually admitted to using trickery to produce rapping noises they attributed to the spirit of a murdered peddler. Still, the sisters Fox were terrific at public relations: their "Spiritualist" society attracted enormous interest, and from the 1850s through the 1870s séances invoking spirits of the dead became outrageously popular in society. Fame gave way to notoriety as skeptics entered the picture and exposed the Foxes. The huge interest in spiritualism was all but ended by 1920.

Today we fast approach the millennium: whether you believe in them or not, those who call themselves mediums are again surfacing in small towns and big cities all over this country. Mediumship has seen an enormous resurgence in popularity among the rich and the famous, not to mention the sober, the sane, and the well educated. Why?

The last great religious revival in America took place in the early fifties when church and synagogue attendance was at its peak. But the bulk of the baby boomers came of age in the sixties—and they weren't having any of it. They took for granted nothing handed down from their parents—which led to the excesses of the sixties and seventies and all the *stuff* you could buy with money.

All of a sudden, in the mid-nineties, came a revival of interest in spirituality—spurred by those boomers, now closer to judgment day than farther from—the same ones who weren't having any of it. With a difference.

No longer interested in singing one-hundred-year-old hymns, the boomers are now looking for a different kind of spirit, a more palpable sense of connection with an afterlife. And aside from the boomers, there is perhaps a deep subliminal longing in all of us that's part of millennium fever—a need to look elsewhere to satisfy that spiritual longing. At a time when many of the old institutions are breaking down, when rigid dogmas are found wanting, when outmoded political systems are found to be dysfunctional—interest in the unexplainable is on the rise in mainstream America. Enter mediumship—among the other paranormal disciplines.

We now know that there are remarkable new ways of looking at the universe and at mysterious occurrences like telepathy, miraculous healings, and the sensitivities of certain people. We now know that even Bill and Hillary Clinton derive rich, spiritual meaning from many—not just Methodist—sources. We also know that if the extraordinary talents of mediums do exist, they certainly can't be explained by modern science's worldview—although quantum physics is slowly taking us closer even to that.

Mediums and psychics are often lumped together, and understandably so, because the lines between the two blur and their similarities are strong. Most mediums say they are definitely psychic, and many psychics work as professional mediums. The greatest distinction between psychics and mediums seems to lie in the professed ability of mediums to contact the spirits of the dead in order to obtain information about the living—and mediums' *primary* work consists of conveying that information back and forth. The very word "medium" implies that the communication between the living and the dead must take place through a third party—the *medium,* or the one in the middle.

Perhaps there is a place in the universe for soul and spirit and other forms of consciousness. Perhaps other generations down the road will wonder at our closed-mindedness.

Perhaps not.

How do you get to be a medium? As New York medium Suzanne Northrup says, "What did *you* want to be when you grew up? Talking to dead folks was not *my* ambition." Most mediums say that ambition had nothing to do with it; rather, something happened when they were children to tell them they had strange powers that enabled them to be witness to an unseen world.

Sometimes, physical trauma like a head blow, a near death experience, or a deep emotional shock can bring on a medium's powers at any age. However it first appears, most mediums say that the talent is genetic and many people in their families "were different" and had psychic powers.

Although some mediums remain awake and alert during a reading, sometimes messages from the dead are given when the medium is in a trance or dream state. This has historical precedence: the Greek oracles at Delphi produced dreamlike states with drug-induced vapors, says psychic Mary T. Browne, and Native Americans use hypnosis, music, and other rituals to produce visions and open a window to the spirit world.

Whatever. *I* needed to try it.

MARISA ANDERSON

A friend with stars in her eyes raves about Marisa Anderson, a medium in Scarsdale, an affluent New York suburb. It's a long ride out. I get a little lost, and I swear I can hear my mom laughing at my terrible sense of direction, as she used to do when I got the two of us terribly tangled as we drove. Finally I arrive. A condominium? A medium lives in a Scarsdale condominium?

The lamps are soft, Tiffany affairs, the apartment is crowded with deco statues, crystal chandeliers, curvy sculptures, a parakeet, an African parrot, and a big, old, fat, orange tabby. The parrot is sitting outside his cage; I'm not too thrilled about that. Marisa's lovely, russet haired and slim, and she directs me to an opposite chair.

There are, she tells me softly, many things in this world of which we cannot dream, and she urges me to try to relax and keep an open mind, urges me to believe I can't anticipate every outcome.

"If you know the play," she asks, "why bother living it?"

Then she gets to work. First she takes my mother's ring from my finger.

"She wasn't wearing this when she died," she announces. "She had trouble with her lung. And I can barely move the fingers of my left hand—hers hurt so much."

I've stopped breathing. She's right on every count.

"Mom was alone when she died," says Marisa.

Wrong.

"Then, why did she feel so isolated, so separated?"

There's something to what she says. When my mother died, she was with Audrey, the young woman who cared for her. But her marriage of fifty years had been terrible, and my father, helpless, as usual, to express his feelings, sat in another room during her brief dying. Was that why she felt isolated? Still, I think Marisa's made a lucky guess.

"Who's down south that she's worried about?" asks the medium.

Nobody. She didn't know anyone down south.

"Well, who's in Florida, then?" demands Marisa, somewhat annoyed.

Oh, wow. Her one remaining sister, Perle, lives in Florida. I forget Florida was in the South. She always worried about Perle.

"*How* are you doing this?" I ask, dumbfounded.

"Spirits exist," says Marisa, "because only matter, not energy, disappears at death. They shoot information through to me by vibrations, and anyone, even you, can learn to pick up the vibrations: it's like turning up the volume on the radio so you can hear it. A hundred years ago," says Marisa, "you would have thought I was a crackpot if I said that little black box there, your tape recorder, would pick up my voice and you could listen to it later when I'm not around. In another hundred years, it won't sound so crazy that I can pick up spirit voices."

The medium's batting a thousand—but then she says a few wrong things.

"I'm getting someone with a Joe, a Joseph. I'm getting a Michael. You have to go to California. I see a miscarriage—did she have a miscarriage?"

Not as far as I know: it's not possible my mom wouldn't have told me that. Then Marisa's correct on a few things, but they're so general, they could be true of anyone.

"Your mom was very proud of you: she wanted you to fulfill everything she couldn't do herself. She liked to travel. Keep wearing her ring; she likes that a lot."

Marisa tells me not to drive a light-colored car on an upcoming trip to Houston because she sees an accident with a light-colored car. She tells me she sees a slight intestinal illness coming up for me. She was right, but did I will it on myself, a self-fulfilling prophecy? She tells me my mother is very worried about something to do with Hawaii. (Wrong. As far as I know, my mother never gave Hawaii two minutes' thought.) She tells me that someone named Frank . . . or Fran . . . or Frances is with my mom. There *was* a beloved sister named Frances who died before her.

This way and that way; I swing from "*How* did she know that?" to "*Wrong, wrong, wrong.*"

When I get home I tally up the things she said that were right (nine—great guesses?), questionable (seven), wrong (five).

So what do I do with this information? Well, one thing I'll *not* do is rent a light-colored car in Houston. I still feel pretty far from my mom. This is what I want to know: If my mother was hovering in spirit in Marisa's condominium, how come she didn't give me a little lecture, tell me one last thing I should do . . . like "wear the pearls"? I mean, then I would have really known. But there was no lecture for me, and that wasn't like my mother at all.

So I don't think my mom was in Scarsdale; still, it was pretty weird.

TOM TROTTA

I remain a skeptic—but maybe slightly chastened. And I'm on my way to Tom Trotta, recommended by the astrologer of a friend of a friend who knows about these things. He's a licensed interfaith minister from Glen Cove, New York, and he's given me specific directions on the telephone: I'm to come with five or six photographs of people who were close to my mom, and I'm to have their birth dates ready. Later, Tom tells me that the birth dates have no astrological significance, they're just something he needs to focus his attention—he doesn't understand it himself. He's forty-four, blue eyed, cute, wearing a turquoise T-shirt, and he looks as if he's about to run a marathon—not contact spirits.

When I arrive I'm sure my mom won't appear because the simple room in which we sit is filled with crosses and religious Christian artifacts. There's a photograph of St. Francis of Assisi and one of the Shroud of Turin, as well as one of Padre Pio, Tom's "spirit protector." This is *definitely* not my mom's kind of place: she was an observant Jew.

Tom is warm and friendly—for about five minutes. Then, when he's ready to begin, he gets a little scary. He goes into a sort of trance and chants to someone (Padre Pio, he later tells me):

"Surround us with the white light of protection, ground us to the center of the earth, allow only that which is of the highest vibration and light to come into this place, *try not to move around so much in that chair because it breaks my concentration!*"

Admonished, I don't move, feeling an uncontrollable urge to giggle. Then he begins, now shooting out each question and statement with an odd urgency.

"Were there any diabetics in your family? What is the birthday of the mother's first child?"

I start to tell him that I'm her only child, but he shoots out, *"The first child, the first child!"*

So I tell him my birthday.

And then the strangest thing. He begins to invoke what sounds like Latin prayers—Latin? No, they're something else. He's chanting in a monotone, and then I know: he's speaking in *tongues,* a strange, incomprehensible language, typically uttered during moments of religious ecstasy. Later Tom confirms this: he says that he doesn't realize it's happening because he goes into a state of altered consciousness and words no longer express what he's hearing. He tells me he's seeing "abstractions" of the "essence" of my mother's spirit. I've read about talking in tongues, but I've never heard it. It's very strange, but after he returns to this chant many times during our hour together, I get used to it—and almost feel soothed by the unfamiliar cadences.

"Who is Fran or Frances?"

This is the second medium who's mentioned my aunt Frances's name, and if my mother is with her, it reassures me enormously.

"You can come out, come out from the second tier," Tom chants. *"You can come, you can come. Who is* H-a-r-i-s," he spells, *"and R? And who is Rose? They have their arms around your mother."*

Now I am deeply shocked. Harris (okay, he got the wrong spelling) and Rachel were my mother's parents, and Rose was her grandmother. There is no way on earth he could have known that. Again he speaks in tongues. Then:

"Who are you, who are you? You must come closer. What is 1921, 1921?"

I haven't a clue.

"Chest gave problems. Who is Audrey, she speaks of Audrey."

Okay. I can no longer throw all this stuff out the window. Audrey Plummer is the young woman in whose arms my mother died.

"Did mother ever lose child?"

Again.

"Who is Julie, Julius, Jules, Julia, Julian, Juland? There's something about a child named like this. Who is it?"

I don't know. (But in nine months my son, Adam, and his wife, Susan, give birth to a daughter. They name her Julia, taking the J from my mother's name. I had not told them of this reading.)

"Your mother in control seat, her heart is very soft, but do what she tells you to do."

Then he's off my mom and on to other stuff.

"What is your connection to Boston, Mass.? When you see man with cuff link and initial of gold, onyx color in ring of gold, when he speaks to you in office, listen to him for benefit."

I listen, heart pounding. (No connection with Boston or a jewelry-laden man ever arises; maybe it will.) Tom alternates predictions with (mostly accurate) descriptions of me— *"You are dominant force, would take sword to cut you away from work"*—to descriptions of my son— *"Sensitive heart, weak knee"* (true).

Then, *"Who is Beth?"* he demands.

It is my daughter's middle name.

"Conflicts with her, but great, great love, such great love. The years will bring closeness and more closeness. Who is Steven?"

It is her husband. I can't talk. And the medium goes on in such detail, such perfect truth, and I can't tell you what he said next, but he was right.

"Who has a white dog?"

No one (although in a year I was to get a white dog).

He says many more things, some totally inaccurate.

Then he asks to look at the photos I've brought. He touches them, caresses the paper faces, and proceeds to analyze (almost perfectly) each person.

"Who is this 'P'?" he asks as he points to my mother's sister, Perle. *"Your mother will come for her within the year."*

In six months my aunt Perle was dead.

"Turn off tape, we're done."

I taped this session, and I've read it back word for word many times. This man has come up with *names* and information that's hidden only in my heart. It's enough to make a skeptic wince.

Was my mother there? There were no messages from her, only descriptions of her. But—her parents and her grandmother, a little old lady who never left Russia—with their arms around her? And blue-eyed Julia?

DIANNE ARCANGEL

The next experience is nothing short of fascinating. I fly to Houston for a session with a woman whose name, her real name—believe it—is Dianne Arcangel. She's a disciple of Raymond Moody, M.D., author of the best-selling *Life after Life*. Dr. Moody is probably the most well-known authority on the study of people who have contacted apparitions of the dead. It is he who has retrieved the primeval practice of mirror gazing, an action the early Greeks and other ancients used as conduits to the gods, the spirit world, and even the future. Over the ages, mystics have always encouraged believers to use a variety of reflective surfaces to connect with departed ones. These range from staring into the still waters of ponds and lakes to gazing into polished metal cauldrons, crystal balls, and other surfaces into which one may *deeply* see. Even mythology has always been filled with examples of mirror gazing: the wicked stepmother chants "Mirror, mirror, on the wall . . ." and sees in the mirror the image of Snow White as the fairest of them all. Aladdin polishes his lamp for its shining, clear depth to reveal the genie.

I read in my research books that Dr. Moody has devised a modern-day version of what the early Greeks and he call a *psychomanteum*. It's a small booth, usually a corner of a room partitioned off into what might be described as a pitch black tent, exactly three feet wide and six feet long. The tent, through which no light can penetrate, is constructed of natural black velveteen cotton, and upon entering, as a flap of the material is pulled to one side, one might notice a three-foot-wide-by-eighteen-inch-tall mirror mounted on the wall at a height that precludes one's seeing her own reflection as she sits in a comfortable, pillow-laden easy chair.

If I were to visit a psychomanteum, is it possible I might see my mom in the mirror? According to Dr. Moody, over half of a group of three hundred people *have* seen apparitions in his psychomanteum, and he refers me to practitioner Dianne Arcangel, telling me that she's had even greater success with her own psychomanteum. I make an appointment to see her.

Dianne sends me a list of instructions: I must eat lightly on the day of our visit, wear loose-fitting clothing of a natural fiber and no watch or perfume (even perfumed deodorant is forbidden), in order to keep things pure and natural. My husband, Larry, comes along to Houston for the ride.

My further instructions are to relax for two days before mirror-gazing day to prepare my mind and body. I go for a swim in the hotel pool: exercise is very conducive to relaxation, Dianne says. As I swim, I think of my mother (something else I'm supposed to do), and from nowhere comes the melody and long-forgotten words of an infant lullaby I haven't thought of for decades. I hear my mother as I do my laps, her crazy, high-pitched little singing voice, and I swear I feel her cool hands on my head—and that's so good. For the first time since she died, I get back the youthful, funny mom instead of the angry old lady in the wheelchair.

In the morning, before we leave to see Dianne, Larry and I make love. I don't know if I'm allowed, I murmur. You're allowed, you're allowed, it's exercise, he assures me.

Dianne (who isn't a medium) calls herself a *facilitator* who helps people make connections with the dead; she's a blond, young forty-five or so, with a grin as wide as Texas, and she embraces me at her door with a welcome that feels real. She works in a hospice center caring for the dying and is closely affiliated with Elisabeth Kübler-Ross, the famed guru of death and dying. We spend a couple of hours talking about my mom and me; I show her pictures and jewelry and my mother's eyeglasses I've brought along, and soon I feel as if Dianne has known us both forever. She tells me that memory has psychic energy and, as I remember things, the loved spirit can seize and hold on to them. She tells me not to worry if I don't see my mother in the psychomanteum mirror—that I will still come out with wisdom that I didn't have when I went in.

I confide my worst fear: how will I be able to sit still in a dark room for a *whole* hour or more? I'll get so bored—not even a book to dip into—I'll die. She laughs, tells me that the experience will seem to fly by (she's right), and then it's time.

But first she asks if my mother had trouble breathing because her own chest feels so heavy. Yes! My mother had trouble breathing ever since the surgery in which she lost a lobe of her lung. And every single psychic is to make some mention of this breathing thing.

Arcangel closes the door and sends me off with a lovely tintinnabulation of some temple bells.

I'm alone in the inky black, save for a tiny lamp with a fifteen-watt bulb placed on the floor in back of me. I squiggle myself until I'm comfortable in the easy chair.

Let me cut to the chase: this is what happened.

Gradually I think I see, at the end of a long, dark road, the outlines of my mother's nose. And my childhood bed. And distant letters reading N O T Y E T. But then, I decide, wanting so much to see her, I must have made it up. What I *know* I didn't make up is a fabulous chartreuse light, sparkling with Fourth of July intensity—brilliant, teeny-tiny light flashes peeling away a corner of the road, gradually peeling back, peeling back the side of the road as if it were a curtain. Then a plane flies over Dianne Arcangel's house and the light goes out, for me. And then comes back. But the road won't peel itself back enough for me to see what's behind it.

It seems so *corny*, such a cliché, that even in that small, dark room, all by myself, I have to smile. I mean, everyone who feels she's transcended death reports the seeing of lights at the end of a tunnel. I think of Robert Lowell's remark, that if we see "a light at the end of the tunnel—it's the light of an oncoming train"—and giggle. But here are those lights—exquisite, prism-shooting lights, and that color—*chartreuse*! I love it.

Later, Dianne said that the seeing of lights is indeed a sacred experience, and green is a symbol of growth. Whose growth—mine? My mom's? I don't know.

So what wisdom do I have that I didn't have before? Well, for one thing, I now know I can sit quietly for a long time—just sit. I've always pooh-poohed meditation as a means to a raised consciousness because I'm always on the move, on the *move*—and at the prospect of simply sitting—and concentrating on an inner vision—I always tended to get very nervous. But maybe this is not engraved in stone, after all. Maybe there's room for some quiet bliss in my life. If, of course, I was sure I wanted quiet bliss. Which I'm not.

And something else: Since the psychomanteum, I seem to think more about other energies out there. Is it possible that memory has an energy of its own, one that doesn't know boundaries? Can I remember, for example, what I never experienced? After the psychomanteum I've been sensing my mom as a very young person—younger than when I ever knew her: she was thirty-two when I was born, but I swear I now sometimes see the twenty-year-old Jane, the eighteen-year-old Jane. I feel that I can remember a mom I never got to know, my gutsier, funnier girl-mom, the mom-before-Sherry, the mom-who-didn't-live-through-Sherry, the *romantic* mom, and that feeling, true or not, inexplicably brings me closer to her. Is this a new wisdom? Who knows.

After arriving home, I asked my ophthalmologist if it could have been an ocular disturbance—the seeing of those sparkly chartreuse lights while staring into a mirror from a darkened room. He doubted it. He also doubted that I'd had a paranormal experience.

So I really didn't find Mom in Houston—well, maybe I did. There was that lullaby. And her nose. And I keep thinking about that spectacular light. But am I stretching it?

ROSEMARY ALTEA

Finally, Rosemary.

I'd heard about her from several people, but she lives in a tiny town in England. No problem: she can do a telephone reading.

Six months ago I would have hooted—spirits by phone? Now, though, I dial her number with my heart in my mouth.

Rosemary Altea is soft-spoken and funny. Thirteen years ago the spirit of a 150-year-old "crazy Apache chief" named Grey Eagle entered her body, and since then the two have been tight—with Grey Eagle being the intermediary between Rosemary and the spirit world. He taught her that spirits are real, that life on this plane lasts just a blink of an eye, but we are all of us eternal and we go on living forever.

When I ask her, as I was told to do, if anyone is trying to reach me, she pauses for a pregnant moment and says reassuringly, "Well, I'm sure there must be."

My instructions are to tell Rosemary whom I hope to reach—

but that's all; she wants absolutely no details about me or my mom or anyone else connected to us. All I am to do is answer "Yes" if what she says seems to make sense to me and "No" if I think she's off base. I am *not* to say "Uh-huh" or "Uh-uh" as Americans, she declares, are wont to do because that drives her bananas.

And she starts.

"Is there a connection to boats and fishing in your life?" asks Rosemary.

Knockout—first try. My husband is a serious fisherman, and I've just written a book called *Secrets of a Very Good Marriage: Lessons from the Sea,* which is all about fishing, boats, marriage, and me. The book has not been published in Britain, and it's highly unlikely that Rosemary has seen it.

"Big fish," Rosemary adds, "*whoppers*—not those tippy little things."

Precisely. It's giant tuna and shark we're after (mostly Larry is after).

"I have a gentleman here," says Rosemary after a while, "and wait—here's your mum with him. He's very thin, he's wearing a funny golf cap, he's a real character, and he's telling you to 'keep cool.' "

My uncle Eli—exactly. Just what he wore, just what he always said, just where he'd be, with my mother.

"And your mum—she's very emotional, she's crying, but very happy, at last, she says. She can *breathe* [that lung again]. She tells me that you're so like her, but you always clashed—and she's sorry, now, she's sorry she put all that guilt on you."

"So how come she didn't admit that when she was alive?" I ask weakly.

"Well," starts Rosemary, "when you pop your clogs—which is an old Yorkshire term for passing into the spirit world . . ."

But I start to laugh at the expression, thinking of my little Orthodox Jewish mom popping her clogs, and Rosemary chuckles also and apologizes for not sounding as spiritual as I might expect.

"When you pop your clogs," she continues, "there's this incredible light—not only a visual light, but *en*lightenment. Your mum says to tell you she's been enlightened."

I wish I could hug my mother. Also, somehow, I think that maybe she wasn't frightened at the moment of her death.

"I'm hearing the name '*John*,' " says Rosemary. "He had problems with his head, his neck? He went quite quickly. He has a great sense of humor—he's grinning at you. 'Send my love to my wife and sister,' he says. 'They're crying for me.' "

Oh, this Rosemary. John was my brother-in-law, and he died from a cancer in his neck, and it went so fast, and I miss his great, good humor. He would have had something scathing and disbelieving to say about my research on this book; rest assured, though, it would have been funny.

My mother—through Rosemary—tells my husband to buy real estate (something she told him to do about once a week when she was alive). She tells me not to "raise my eyebrow" at my daughter (*moi?*) because, doing so, I repeat the pattern of miscommunication from Mom to me to Jennifer. My mom says she wishes I would have let her have this conversation prior to her passing, but I was not ready when she was—and she was not ready when I was. Don't make the same mistake with your own daughter, warns my mom, Jane.

Rosemary tells me that I will write another book connected to the last and it will be very successful and she can't wait to read it. My mother, through Rosemary, says, "You are my heart and all I have."

My mother said that a lot. Exactly that.

But then Rosemary says she hears my mother call me "my darling, my darling . . ."

Well, she never called me "my darling"—so I'm turned off by this bit of dialogue, supposedly from her. This sounds like what Rosemary calls *her* daughter, perhaps. But later, when I tell my friend Margie about this part, Margie says, "Maybe your mother used to *think* 'my darling' but never got the words out when she was alive." Well, maybe.

My mom, through Rosemary, says that she will always walk with me and, like a lantern, guide and protect me; that she has survived death and is just in a different place; that she sends her love to my children; that, Rosemary says, I can feel her breath on my cheek if I concentrate.

I can't. But maybe that's because my cheek is wet with tears.

"One of the greatest pains to human nature is the pain of a new idea," wrote an English social scientist named Walter Bagehot in the mid–nineteenth century.

I'm not finished with this new idea, not finished looking for Mom. I've got to go further—to places I've never before gone. Safe journey, Sherry. This is turning out not to be the silly lark I envisioned.

Keep posted.

Psychics

A friend of mine had a schizophrenic sister who saw visions, heard voices, went into trancelike states, and occasionally felt taken over by spirits. She was a mess. Twenty years after meeting this unfortunate soul, I realize that the description of psychics (who also see visions, hear voices, sometimes go into trances, and are occasionally taken over by spirits) almost exactly meets her medical symptoms.

Almost. If God is in the details, He (or She) is also in the differences. Most important difference between a schizophrenic and a psychic? Most psychics are not disturbed people. They look like you, they look like me, they go to the opera, they go to the movies, they make meat loaf and ski at Aspen. They manage their finances, have successful personal relationships, and some even have public relations agents working on their behalf. Another big difference: Psychics can control their "trance" states, while the families of schizophrenics only wish they could do the same.

Psychics, like mediums, also seem to have known about their talents since childhood, or else they've triggered their abilities through trauma. Some psychics are *unwillingly* gifted, and they hate their powers; their experiences frighten them (especially precognitive dreams about disaster or death), and they often feel isolated from "normal" people, sometimes even fearing for their own sanity. Most, however, learn to adjust to the way they sense or retrieve knowledge about their own and others' lives, and many make it a well-paying career.

Psychics, unlike mediums, usually do not communicate with the dead: they're people who just know unknowable things—even without dealing with the dead. The word "psychic" derives from the Greek *psyche,* meaning "soul": a psychic claims she has the exceptional ability *to acquire information by extrasensory means* about the human soul or mind or even about events that will happen. It is thought by many that everyone has these extraordinary psychic abilities just waiting to be developed. How does a psychic know your sister will break her ankle in a week—or your boyfriend, who has never written a poem, will? She just does.

Some psychics claim to be able to affect objects with psychokinesis (PK). Probably the most famous is the Israeli psychic Uri Geller, who can bend metal objects by stroking or looking at them; he can start or stop watches in the same way. For this reason, such PK phenomena are often called "the Geller Effect."

Famed psychics abound. Edgar Cayce (who died in 1945, leaving literally thousands of followers) was the noted psychic whose prophecies and healings continue to baffle scientists and other trained investigators. Cayce, who had no medical training, was able to diagnose and prescribe treatment and surgery (using serums and medicines not yet invented) for people he'd never met, who lived great distances from him. He predicted the date of the end of World War II, the growth of nonexistent seaports, the end of Communism in Russia, and the 1929 Wall Street crash; he could accurately name the whereabouts of lost objects he'd never seen and, while in a trance, speak foreign languages he'd never studied.

Psychic ability (particularly the use of ESP) gains new credibility as parapsychologists study ESP in the laboratory under rigid scientific controls. Researchers like Richard S. Broughton, Ph.D., director of research at the Institute for Parapsychology in Durham, North Carolina, are generally dubious, though, about storefront psychics, psychic detectives, and psychic business consultants; Broughton says these "professions" lie somewhere between harmless hucksterism and shameless exploitation. Still, he hastens to add that their veracity is no longer an issue that can be dismissed out of hand because all the evidence is not yet in.

Throughout recorded history psychics have been called many things, including prophets, seers, soothsayers, witches, priests and priestesses, sorcerers and shamans. They've also been called fakes.

Can a real psychic tell you what's in store for you?

Would you believe she was psychic if she did?

What *would* it take for you to believe in psychic ability?

Well, I'm going to find out what it takes for me to search for my mom through psychics.

The Psychics

MARY T. BROWNE

WOODY ALLEN SAID, "There is no question that there is an unseen world. The problem is, how far is it from midtown and how late is it open?"

Well, at the very least, I know that it's not very far from the cozy Greenwich Village living room of, arguably, New York's most famous psychic, while Mary T. Browne argues with the producer of a famous talk show on the telephone: No, she will *not* say what the producer wants her to say if she makes a guest appearance on the show. No, she will not change her mind. Yes, she *will* forget about going on the show, if that's how they want it.

I'm glad to have the few moments to myself to look around.

The intimate room is dominated by an enormous painting of a green-tinted Madame Helena Petrovna Blavatsky, the legendary Russian-born Theosophist who is Browne's heroine. Blavatsky's holding a flirty fan, and her weird gaze is staring me down, no question about that: Madame wins and I look away. Lush wing chairs, Tiffany lamps with fringed shades, exposed brick walls, lace curtains at the windows, wicker baskets plopped with purple pansies, mauve and gray everywhere—this apartment is definitely, with apologies to Bette Davis, *not* a dump. No incense, no candles, no Gregorian chants; a real person lives here, I think.

"Your worst fear is that you'll outlive your husband," says a husky voice. "Don't worry—you're going to pass from this earth within six months of each other."

God. We haven't even said hello yet. And she's right about the worst fear part.

Mary T. stands in front of me: stunning navy dress with gold buttons, great Anna Wintour haircut, intense blue eyes, tomato red lipstick, and a voice that trills and vibrates. "I'm like a radio," she says. "My body just picks up waves and thought patterns. Sometimes the information comes to me in words through my head, and sometimes I see a giant screen with the information on it—but wherever it's coming from, it's a spiritual place. This is called claircognizance. Look—some people do chocolate-chip cookies; I pick up."

She has a steady, unwavering gaze, and I feel like a deer caught in her headlights; she's *funny,* too. A funny, pretty psychic: can such things be?

Browne is the author of *Life After Death,* and I have heard about her from the growing network of people who've started to delve into the mysteries of the paranormal: her clients include Wall Street tycoons, psychiatrists, purse designers, and theatrical and publishing types, as well as dentists, lawyers, and secretaries.

She's Irish bred but Iowa born and first learned she was psychic when she was seven and left to answer phones at Aunt Mame's funeral parlor in Iowa. "I was all by myself," she recalls, "standing in a doorway, and a bunch of roses levitated through the whole room and then went plop back on the little podium right near the coffin. It was then I saw the shadow of a woman smiling and waving at me before she disappeared. I went up to the open coffin and realized that the body there was the same woman I'd just seen; she was showing me there wasn't any real death."

Aside from the fact that one might question the wisdom of

adults who leave a seven-year-old alone in a funeral parlor, it doesn't seem to have done Mary any harm. As she grew, she had more hints of her sensitivity. "I just used to be able to help my friends find lost stuff, and somehow I just knew what was going to happen to them in the future." Her grandmother told her to keep quiet about her psychic gifts. Even now she's somewhat reluctant to discuss them at length—presumably because most people think you're a lunatic if you look like a model but talk like Madame Blavatsky. Eventually Browne came to New York to study with Stella Adler and become a singer and an actress; while waiting for casting calls, she did short psychic readings for the other would-be stars—and soon realized she couldn't fight her true calling.

I get a neat, short lecture.

"Since the beginning of time, there have been psychics," she tells me. "It's a gift—like Pavarotti's voice. It takes a good deal of feminine sensitivity to be a psychic who can see in another dimension—that's why the best ones are usually women or gay men. My opinion, anyway. A good psychic sees past, present, and future. I sense what's going on around people, what's coming in the future, what's affecting them most deeply from the past. I am not a channeler—a channeler is someone who becomes someone else. I'd change the channel—give me FM—if that happened. And anyone who calls the Psychic Friends Network deserves what he gets. Who *are* those people? I wouldn't call the Dermatologists Network if I had a skin disease. I'd go to the AMA or get a referral from a friend. You only go to a psychic who's been recommended.

"Most people go to a psychic for hope, some come out of despair, some out of curiosity. *You*—you come because you want to *not* believe. Right? We'll see.

"Watch what you put in your stomach. You put an awful lot of junk in your mouth."

Does she mean the M&M's, the endless licorice? Has she been following me?

"Back to your husband," says Mary T. "You've been married to him before because you could not learn to love that deeply in one life. He helps you cool your jets. When you met him, it was a case of instant recognition: it's as if you were taught a karmic lesson that you remembered—*This is Larry, grab him back for yet another life!* Look—these things are planned. If you feel like being allegorical, think of the character Frankie in Carson McCullers's *Member of the Wedding* who wanted to find the "we of me"; you and Larry are, for each other, the "we of me." Now wait a minute, Larry's a Cancer, isn't he—he finds a God force on the water—he must have been a Portuguese fisherman in another life, likes to be the captain of his own ship—right?"

So what else is new?

Mary's sitting in a wing chair, I'm on the couch, legs curled under me as if I'm on *my* couch. I feel at home here.

"You rebel from your mother in your need to move mountains," she says (not asks, *says*). "Your mother wished a lot. You insist on *doing* it. On the other hand, your husband is better at reflecting. He taught you to find the beauty of the spirit in the calm of the sea."

Well, I'm working on it. Finding the calm part.

"Have his blood sugar tested," says Mary T. "And, there's something funny going on with your hip. It's not aligned properly."

Neither of these two statements is meaningful to me. Maybe they *will* be. My hip feels fine, and I'm not about to go to a doctor to check out a hip that doesn't hurt. I did make Larry have his blood sugar tested and it's fine.

"Who was born colic-y to teach you patience?" she demands. I know.

"Your son will have a transition soon. He's a writer? . . .

No? . . . You say he's a lawyer? Well, he could have been a contender in the writing field if he'd chosen the road less traveled."

Oh, God—I'm overcome with guilt. Who encouraged him to become a lawyer? *Moi.*

"Well, he will attract creative clients because he's very creative. He still *might* also be a contender in the writing field. In some way, this young man will see great success. He and you are totally aspected. Along with your mother."

Whatever "aspected" means, she's right: he and I were born on the same day. Along with my mother. And how does she know I have a son, anyway? She didn't even ask. She must be bugging my phone. I decide I'm overreacting.

"Do you still want to *not* believe?" she says.

I prefer not to answer and put my journalist cap back on by asking Mary T. if she communicates with the dead.

"Almost never. *Jamais!* Look—highly developed spirits are not earthbound, so they're not talking. We must not try to pull them back to the earth plane or drag them back to the physical when their souls should be left serene. Most people we know are going to be real happy on the other side, eventually. So who would we be talking to, here—suicides, still undeveloped souls who can't yet leave the earth? Once in a while I do get a message from a beloved person who knows *you're* going to be fine but just wants to say good-bye—but I haven't done the contacting."

Then she looks at me intently. "Slow down," she warns. "You're the fastest gun in the West. You think that's so terrific?

"You have good friends now," Mary T. tells me. "But you will soon find the marvelous in the midst of the mundane."

I love that. It means many things to me, on many levels—the marvelous in the midst of the mundane. I choose to believe it's so.

The reading continues. I've been to enough "sensitives" by now, and I'm not shocked out of my socks when she hits—just as

I try not to discount the future events she talks of that are not yet provable. At one point I complain to Mary T.—how can I, how can she, be *sure* she's right about what she sees in the future? It's all such a mystery.

"I like to take the mystery out and leave the miraculous intact," she says.

And I leave it at that.

BETTINA

I've been hearing about her. I go out to lunch with an NBC news executive, and when I tell her about my book she gets very excited.

"You *must* try to find Bettina I-Don't-Remember-Her-Last-Name. Years ago she told me I'd meet the man of my dreams in two days, and I did. She is *great* at predicting what will happen!"

How do I find her? Another colleague, who also doesn't remember Bettina's last name, tells me she's heard that the psychic helped a media baron build his television empire.

I really doubt this. Still, since it's the only lead I have, I dial the media baron's offices and ask the secretary if she knows anything about all this. Miraculously, after some whispered consultation, someone else comes on the line to give me Bettina's number. Hmmm.

When I call to make an appointment, her secretary tells me to bring photographs and a check. This is the most expensive paranormal practitioner I've yet encountered—two hundred dollars a half hour, more than my orthopedist. In line with my decision to be honest about who I am, I tell the secretary I'm a writer.

Bettina lives in a high-rise on New York's Upper East Side. *Very* fancy: apparently the psychic business is fruitful. The concierge announces me, and I rise in a golden elevator. Her apartment is expensively furnished, and her terrace overlooks the world. On the wall are photographs of her grandson and her theatrical-looking daughter (also psychic; it runs in the family). I'm told to wait, so I sink into an overstuffed sofa, under a standing lamp topped with a heavily crystal-beaded lampshade, and I browse through her coffee table scrapbook—a compendium of letters from satisfied customers and magazine articles written about her.

The secretary tells me the psychic's ready.

Bettina's an artist's sketch—big and blond with a baby's pink-and-white complexion; she's wearing teenager bangs, a rhinestone barrette, and a pink sweatshirt that says "PARIS." Sitting at a small, square card table, she beckons me to sit opposite and give her my photographs, which she spreads out on the table.

"Have you written a screenplay?" she asks.

No, wrong kind of writing.

"Well, sweetheart, you will," she informs me.

"Is this your husband—he's a doctor?" she asks as she lightly scratches the photograph to pick up his energy.

Yes, he's my husband, and no, he's not a doctor.

"Well, he *would* have been a great doctor," she says, and smiles. I'll give her that.

"He's got a back problem, a slight curvature," she says. No, he doesn't. "Well, he *will,*" she says. "And he's having some difficulties with his teeth."

("So what sixty-year-old *doesn't* have difficulties with his teeth?" asks my husband defensively when I tell him later.)

"Who's Steven?" she asks abruptly. It is my son-in-law. "Nice guy," she comments. I'll give her that, too.

"He's in communications?" she asks. Bingo—he *is* in radio. That's pretty good, Bettina, I think. I don't think I've ever written about it, so she couldn't have researched that bit. Bettina seems very happy when she gets something right. "He's going to expand, make some big changes, but he better be careful with the stock market." I make a mental note to tell Steve, even as I know Steve's going to give me a seriously dubious look.

Then she drops about ten wrong names. "Who's Ruth, Jack or Joe, Stan or Sid Silverman?"

Sid Silverman? No one I know. "Let it go," says Bettina.

"Your son is Adam?" she asks, scratching Adam's photo. "He's very creative and will start a new undertaking soon. He's a great guy." I wonder if Bettina ever told anyone her son was *not* a great guy—indeed, he was an ax murderer. Sure, I'm impressed with her knowing the name, and sure, she did repeat what Mary T. Browne said about Adam's being creative, but a bad voice in my head still tells me she may have read about Adam in articles I've written. Then I stop myself: I'm being unfair. Maybe she's really a "sensitive."

"And this is your daughter-in-law?" she asks, scratching at a picture of a pretty bride who is very fair and looks nothing like me. Lucky guess, I'd say.

"She's pregnant," Bettina announces. Bettina's right. Not bad. "If it's a boy, she will probably name her child with a 'J'—maybe Jeff or Jason," she says. That gives me a little tug of the heart because my mother was Jane and I've been hoping Sue and Adam will name their baby after her.

I notice that Bettina looks deeply and sharply at me. Whenever she says something tentatively—for example, "You got along very well with your mother"—she watches me; and now she must see my body language negate her words because she instantly changes that to "Your mother was very strong, very difficult, right?"

Then: "You have an analytical mind, sweetheart," she tells me.

I think I hate this $200 reading. Still, I don't want to hurt her feelings. "You have a silver car," she announces. I start to say no, but she, watching me, quickly interjects, "Blue—a *blue* car?" Yes. "I want the wheel alignment checked," she says. Disbelieving, I nevertheless make a mental note to check the wheel.

Then she says a few startling things.

"Did you fix your mother's ring, sweetheart?"

Now, no one knows I have my mom's wedding ring, broken, in a drawer in my home. "She wants you to fix it," says Bettina. "And do you have her dishes?" I do. "Don't break any," she says. It sounds like my mom. "And her fur coat? She wants you to give it to your daughter."

I will, right after the reading.

"Your daughter's in entertainment?"

"No. She's a lawyer," I offer, feeling a little sorry for the psychic. Some investigative journalist.

Well—she'll *get* into entertainment law—probably through her husband," says Bettina. "She's a great gal, a great negotiator."

She points to a picture of Connie, my literary agent.

"Who's this?" she asks. I tell her. "Well, who's this 'Angela' associated with her?"

Now *no one* would know that. Angela is definitely a person in my agent's life.

"Connie's not been feeling well," says Bettina, "but she'll be much better soon. She could sell the Brooklyn Bridge to anyone." True.

"Who's Kathryn, Carol, Christina?"

Beats me. Except, on reflection, Carol *could* be my editor. But, just as quickly, I think, *Who doesn't know a Carol?* A safe bet to throw in a name like Carol.

"Let it go," she says quickly.

"Your husband and you get along . . . ?" she says tentatively, watching me carefully. And, seeing my face, she declares, "Well, you're soul mates, sweetheart, and will be throughout eternity. Did you enjoy my reading?"

And that's how I knew my $200 half hour with the famous psychic was up.

FAITH

Faith, the police psychic, is waiting for me in a secluded room of the local precinct, although the cops will never admit they know her—let alone the fact that they come to her for help. Blond and pretty in her white nurse's uniform (because that's her day job), she's law enforcement's court of last resort, she's the place where they go when all else fails, she's their ace in the hole. Although people like Faith operate quietly all over the country, rarely does anyone in officialdom claim to use a psychic to solve a crime. Only in the comic books, lady.

But also in the station house.

I have friends in high places, and they've led me to Faith. If I reveal her name, I blow it for faith in the Establishment—and also for Faith.

"It's hard for the police, and I can understand that," she explains softly. "In every court in the land, let alone in every police department, they deal in black and white. My work is in a gray area, and gray doesn't hold up in court, so law enforcement can't sanction it openly—no matter how often they see I'm right."

This is what she's often right about:

If she's provided with a photograph or the keys of a homicide victim, she has the ability to create an uncannily accurate personality profile of the killer, an officer (to whom I've promised anonymity) says. She can often tell you what the suspect likes to eat and his most personal habits. If you can give her a photograph of the suspect, "well, I just *know* that person after I look at the picture long enough. I may not get his name, but I can write out a written profile that is anywhere from 80 to 100 percent accurate."

Faith is a police psychic. Born and bred in a small southern town, she didn't ask for her talent, which is a form of clairvoyance—the perception of objects, events, or people that is not discerned through the normal five senses. In Faith's case, her gift is sometimes linked with precognition—an ability to see into the future. She says she found she had this special aptitude when she was about ten and she and her friends would discuss the comic strips in the newspapers: the only difference between Faith and her buddies was that she would always know what *tomorrow's* comic would feature. "How do you do that?" her friends would ask when the strip would appear, as described.

She didn't know. She still doesn't know.

"And I've given up trying to figure it out," she says, smiling. "All I do now is think of myself as a bloodhound trying to pick up a scent—except in my case, it's a *feel*. If the police have a missing woman and I *feel* she's dead, *she always is*. I often can actually see her in a forest or a grave—wherever the body is. If I *feel* her alive, the police better get cracking to find her before that changes.

"My specialty is murder—actually, murdered adults. I don't do well with missing children—they give off a lot of confusing messages and static, and there are others, I know, who are far more productive with kids. I've discovered that I see things in mirror images—so if I see a body in a white house on the right-hand side of the road, I've learned that we have to look for a dark-colored house on the left-hand side of the road. I also often get a sense of the suspect's occupation—like sometimes I'll feel he works in a fast-food restaurant: the next step for the police would be to check out all the neighboring fast-food places."

Apart from her closest friends and family (her two daughters show evidence of her gift, which makes her think there's a genetic aspect to the talent), hardly anyone knows about Faith.

"This is who I am and this is what I do. I don't have a crystal ball, don't wear black, don't look weird, but it's still hard to explain it to people.

"Remember," she says, "this is the Bible Belt and I'm a typical Southern Baptist, born and raised in that religion. A lot of folks liken psychic abilities to the occult, to black magic, and they don't want to know anything about it. Maybe I'd feel the same way if I didn't have the gift."

Because she does consider her psychic ability a gift, Faith is on no one's payroll and sets no private fees. Most of the time she works for free because she feels "I have to give back to the world." She accepts expense money and reward money if her work has succeeded and a reward happens to be offered (she never asks for it). Sometimes a special budget is apportioned just for her, but she never refuses a case if there's no money in it.

She's usually exhausted. She sandwiches in her police work between the nursing that is her family's support, and "make no mistake, this is hard work, draining stuff—not like the flaky stories you see on TV where they'll bring in a 'sensitive' and boom—the case is solved. I've been working steadily on a case now for two and a half years: it occurred in a small, eastern coastal town. Three people were murdered and three badly injured. I know the killer is a loner, he dislikes milk and milk products, he is brilliant, he has trouble maintaining work and personal relationships, he came from an abusive background, and I've drawn a sketch of him—he looks a little like Scottie Pippen. The three survivors absolutely identify the drawing as the suspect. I *know* this guy *intimately,* and still, he eludes me. It's so frustrating."

Faith works only on personal recommendation and for several police departments.

"It's hard for a new department to come to trust me," she says, "and a very high level of trust is needed in this work. When I'm first called in to a new precinct, we all sit around a table and play the game—the game I have to get through before I can convince them I'm on the level, the game in which they test me without calling it a test.

"I can promise you that any investigative agency will *never* give someone who's brought in everything they know about a case. They can't. If there's one smidgen of information that relates to the crime—information that can somehow trap the murderer—and that tidbit is not known to the press—if it gets out, it can blow your whole case. They're careful, and they should be.

"So we sit around this table and I ask for a photo, and then I give them the one bit they're holding back. I love this part—I always can tell when I'm getting close to picking it up because their faces are so readable."

She doesn't talk about her work a whole lot. "Listen, there's one gentleman who's in a state prison for life, and I put him there. If he gets out on parole, I don't want him knocking on my door. That's why very few people know where my door is."

It's getting late and Faith has to go be a nurse. I think she senses some lingering skepticism in me because she says, "Let me help you get through this, Sherry. Let me read *you*. Let's suppose you were a suspect—or, God forbid, a victim. Have you got any keys—I love to pick up stuff from keys. I don't know why, but if I can touch the keys of a victim or suspect, I just *zip* into the future or the past. Maybe it has to do with the magnetic field of the metal, because I don't do as well with material. What do you think?"

I haven't the foggiest. Metal doesn't do it for *me*.

Now, you can either believe or disbelieve what I'm about to tell you, but as Richard Pryor once said, "Who do you believe—me or your lying eyes?" What happened next happened exactly as I tell it here.

I give Faith two keys on a small ring that I have in my purse. They're not my regular klutzy bunch of nine keys (which supply entry to the various houses, mailboxes, and offices of my life), because since I'm in the midst of a research trip for this book, I don't have my regular door-opening needs and I've left the heavier key ring home. Actually this smaller key ring is only two weeks old: I've gotten a new puppy at home and I'm in the midst of housebreaking him, so I've put together a tiny ring of two house keys that I can just grab to throw in my shirt pocket when I go on the three thousand daily walks Augie requires. I keep this small ring of keys on a surface near the front door and I use them *just* for Augie walks.

Faith takes the keys from me and fondles them. She gets a puzzled look on her face—and shakes her head. I ask her what's the matter.

"It's crazy," she says. "It's not working. All I see is a small, tannish white dog with short, stubby legs, and for the life of me, I can't pick up anything about you."

So who do you believe—me or your lyin' eyes? The trouble is that neither Faith nor my eyes are lyin'. This paranormal stuff is starting to get to me.

THE PSYCHIC FAIR

Everyone lives by selling something.
ROBERT LOUIS STEVENSON

So I see this little advertisement in a give-away local newspaper and it says PSYCHIC FAIR: READINGS AND EXPERTS. I'm up for it, so I find the Beverly Hotel in New York City and walk up two grimy flights, and a woman in a purple headband and gypsyish skirt greets me, tells me to sign my name on a mailing list and register for a reading with any one of the eighteen "experts," each sitting neatly before a round table.

Before I do so, I take a little walk around.

Some of the tables are decorated with colored tarot cards laid out carefully, others with wooden beads, candles, burning incense. At each table is a sign with the expert's name—there's Louis, there's Ann, there's Theresa, each dominating her psychic domain. Louis gives me a brochure as I pass that tells me the pain in my "mussels" will disappear with a special reading only he can give me. Ann is leaning in and talking intensely to a Maybelline eye-shadowed, wide-eyed, stud-tongued teenager. I eavesdrop.

". . . and for only ten more dollars, I can give you a *personal* potion that will ensnare his heart," I hear Ann say, and I want to run and call the teenager's mother to come get her.

I walk around the small room three times. Words waft over from the tables.

"Reconstruct . . ."
        "Allow the poet to come out . . ."
"Connect with spirit . . ."
". . . conjunction in the sky of Uranus and Neptune . . ."
"I see your brother . . ."

A woman in a turban is selling stones and crystals and, unaccountably, pink, round rubber balls. A guy with a yarmulke is selling something suede called "sacred sacs"; when I ask, he tells me that they are protective coverings for my spiritual items. My mother had such a suede thing in which she used to save dimes and quarters for charity. Suddenly I find myself thinking harder of my mother. Could I find her here? No. My mother, as she liked to

say, "was nobody's fool." She could always tell the difference between commerce and sacred sacs.

There's a man and his pretty blond assistant wearing triangles
on their heads as they explain the power of the Pyramids. A guy
from Istanbul is selling an ancient means of cleaning out one's ears
by blowing candle smoke in them. He says the technique was
used by Moses and is unbeatable for earaches. A tour group oper-
ator is pushing trips to "power places" like Stonehenge or the
Pyramids or to see the Oracle at Delphi; he tells me it will be entirely possible to hook up with my past lives in such power spots.
It was hard to resist a pack of cards that promised tips for striking
up conversations with dead people I have known and loved.

The customers who have signed up for readings are almost all
sad looking and ravenous for wise words. Some take notes. Some
tape what their psychic expert tells them.

I approach an attractive, intelligent-looking woman who seems
to be a Native American—she's *dressed* like a Native American,
anyway—sitting at a table that is temporarily empty.

"Are you a mystic?" I ask, thinking that I should just try this.

"I'm an intuitive counselor," she answers.

"What's that?" I ask.

"Whatever," she answers.

I buy a bag of ginger and get out of there.

Weeks later, at an astrological session with Rick Jarow, I ask if he
ever does readings at psychic fairs.

"The salami-and-cheese festivals?" he says, and smiles.

Well then, does it make him angry, all those scam artists per-
verting the psychic highways, making a mockery of his life's work?

"Not at all," he answers. "Look at these happenings as rem-
nants of the destroyed pagan culture. It makes me laugh, I enjoy

it—just as I enjoy David Letterman or Jay Leno—it's people expressing themselves. It's entertainment, it's a festive atmosphere. If they don't maliciously, meanly hurt anyone, what's the harm? The day of the gray flannel suit is over, and people want to *be* the show rather than just watch the show. When Rome was in its decadence, Rome became like a Fellini movie. Think of psychic fairs as a Fellini movie."

Well, okay. But *where* is that young girl's mother?

So?

SO, IT WAS OVER—the first leg of my journey. I was finished looking for Mom through mediums and psychics, anyway.

"Well, did you, did you find your mom?" eagerly asked a dozen people who knew I was looking.

There are three possible answers here:

One—that somehow and somewhere there exists a spirit plane, and my mother's spirit resides there. This is a lovely conceit but frankly, pretty hard to buy for me, my mother's daughter, a serious skeptic.

Two—that her spirit and those of all my lost beloveds really do exist—but in my mind, and the psychics and mediums were somehow able to read my mind—a prospect I no longer find quite so unbelievable.

The third possibility is one I no longer accept: there is nothing. So, there's something. But—what?

I think something of my mom was there in England with Rosemary—and also in Tom Trotta's room and, come to think of it, maybe in some of the other places, too. Look—I'm still not sure, but too many incredible messages have been sent to me; I have to try to park my arrogance—the stuff that says "Impossible."

What would it take for me to be *sure?* For absolute proof, did I need my mom to tell me how to live and what to say and to wear my pearls? She did all that when she was with me—and I hated it.

The funny thing is that I guess there are many ways to get to the place where we can find our mothers; a spirit isn't only pie in the sky or a voice saying "Wear your pearls." So she didn't give me her famous little lecture—or any instructions at all. So I never did really find out if she was frightened when she died.

But: there was this strongest sense of connection. And there were the inexplicable names and knowledge the spiritualists shot at me. And telling Larry to snap up property didn't hurt.

Suddenly I feel that there's more than my mom missing: perhaps I also ought to look for me. If I get to know myself better and figure out for the first time really, what it means to be the daughter to my mother, maybe I'll find a more direct route to her.

There are good people, say my friends who are really into this stuff; they're diviners who can tell me things about my mother and me, about my unremembered self—but especially about things that *will* happen. "Oh, sure," I mutter. But now I must admit that my interest has been piqued.

I plan to try to relinquish control for a while—and just listen, before I judge.

But astrology? Channeling? I hope I don't meet anyone I know on my way in.

Off to look for Sherry.

Part II | Looking for Me

Take your hands off the
steering wheel.
GARY ZUKAV

Astrology

"Beware the ides of March," warned Julius Caesar's astrologer, but *did he listen*—noooooo, darling, as my mother-in-law used to say. Of all the paranormal genres, astrology seems to be the one even skeptics take a *little* seriously. Who among us can resist a peek at his newspaper horoscope even while publicly decrying the ancient practice?

Dr. Eugene Hecht, professor of physics at Adelphi University in New York and a man of pure science, believes that of all the paranormal genres, the closest to having a scientific basis is astrology and that certain predictions made from the planets and the moon and the stars of the horoscopes can probably be explained logically and tested scientifically. "Everyone on the planet is interacting gravitationally," says Dr. Hecht. "There is matter and there is space, and there's no question they interact. The loony bins do go into mayhem on the full moon, the number of suicides do rise on the full moon, the grunions do come up and lay their eggs when there would be a full moon and high tide—even if you take them and put them in a tank in Nicaragua. We are wonderfully connected and bound together in the universe."

Astrology operates on the very principle Dr. Hecht cites—the one that says we *are* all connected, the heavens and everything and everybody on the earth—and being so united, we share a common space and time with the moon, the planets, the sun, and all their interrelationships. These heavenly bodies influence human affairs—our own and all eternity's—and our horoscopes, our "birth charts," plot the energies that flow in our own particular magnetic fields.

Astrology, like tarot readings, numerology, and tea leaf reading, is an art of *divination*—the profession of prophets. More and more of us seem to want to listen to prophets in these last years of the waning century. Whether our hearts warm to Nostradamus or Patrick Walker, we're turning to those who seek to foretell future events or discover hidden knowledge by supernatural means: these people attempt to communicate with *something else out there* in order to learn the will of the gods. They do this either through direct communication with gods or spirits—or through the interpretation of natural signs (like the planets, moon, and stars) or artificial signs (like tarot cards, omens, or portents).

Divination has been popular throughout all of history. Around 3000 B.C. the Babylonians and the ancient Chaldeans studied birds' flights and patterns in water for signs that would foretell the future. The ancient Greeks and Romans didn't make a move without their oracles. In 2000 B.C. the ancient Chinese had court diviners who interpreted sticks (the I Ching), bones, and other objects. In fact, most courts employed royal diviners whose very lives depended on how correct their forecasts were, job fallout with which today's weather diviners don't have to cope.

Traditionally the responsibility for divination has fallen to those who are known especially for their supernatural powers— the priests, prophets, shamans, and witches of the human saga.

But divination has been a factor, even among the traditionally religious. Moses himself was an extraordinary diviner in constant touch with God, who told him how to lead his people from Egypt's bondage. It is part of traditional Christian belief that the Holy Ghost spoke through the diviner prophets who foretold the life and passion of Jesus Christ. Islam recognizes Mohammed as the last and greatest of the diviner prophets.

Today divination still reigns strong in many cultures.

In western Uganda, for example, the priests of the Lugbara tribe have a nasty little divination technique. They fill little pots with medicines that represent those who are suspected of a crime;

then they put the pots on the fire. Whichever pot does *not* boil over points the finger to the guilty person. Some suspects are required to eat disgusting potions or stews; whoever develops the worst indigestion is the guilty guy.

Beyond the religious practitioners, many other types of diviners exist. If *you're* known for your extraordinary intuition, foresight, and perception, perhaps *you're* a diviner. Why not? Surely my aunt Reba, who almost always correctly forecast what my dreams were going to bring, was an expert in the art. In the West, however, some forms of divination are more accepted than others. Tell your colleague you've been to a Gypsy fortune-teller—and watch how funny her face gets. Tell the same colleague you've been to a great astrologer and she'll probably ask for the telephone number.

As I start looking for me in the world of the paranormal, it seems right to begin with the divining art of astrology.

Of all the divination techniques, astrology, as old as measured time, is the most ubiquitous. Fifty thousand years ago the Cro-Magnon people read patterns of stars in the sky, and today even the steadiest, most predictable people seem to have astrologers. My savvy, skeptical attorney friend Linda has an astrologer—although she doesn't like to talk about it and says if I write it, she'll deny it. Queen Elizabeth has an astrologer, as does her ex-daughter-in-law Diana, whose astrologer told her that Charles would never reign as king and her son William will succeed Queen Elizabeth after her death. When they were in the White House, Nancy Reagan and her husband had an astrologer. Saddam Hussein has an astrologer. There's a financial astrologer in New York (Henry Weingarten—see "Resources" section) without whom a large number of Wall Street types don't make a move. Hugh Hefner, Yoko Ono, Goldie Hawn, and Carrie Fisher have astrologers. Psychiatrist Carl Jung thought that astrology was one of the great connectors, sometimes consulting his patients' horoscopes to search for hidden possibilities and problems.

So what exactly is astrology?

Simply, it's the belief that the stars, planets, and sun influence events on the earth; most students of the art feel that astrology is also a means to foretell future earthly events as well as explain past and present ones. What happens in the heavens, say astrologers, is cyclical—it's happened over and over again since time immemorial. These cycles show up in everyday life here on earth as well as in the heavens because the same energies that function in our personal universes also function in the larger universe.

Astrologer William Hewitt says that all of us notice recurring or cycling effects in our lives, "certain habits, problems, and joys seem to occur to us, over and over." Since the celestial bodies exert specific forces and specific personalities, understanding them helps us to use the planetary influences. If we come to recognize the repeating patterns, we can come to see ourselves in greater perspective, see the big picture, as it were. Astrology, say practitioners, gives us a way to notice the cycles in our lives so we can order those lives to our best advantage.

Since these cycles repeat themselves, the heavens serve as a perfect divining tool. By studying the planetary arrangement for a given moment, says Hewitt, the astrologer can gain an accurate picture of what has happened on the earth at that moment. "The planets and their relationships to each other and to the earth change unendingly in an absolutely predictable way," says Hewitt. "We can mathematically calculate exactly where every planet will be at any time in relation to any point on earth. This means we can have a mirror that can reflect events in the past, present, or future anywhere on earth."

There are as many different approaches to astrology as there are practitioners, but the most popular is *natal astrology*. The natal *horoscope* (in Greek *horoscope* means "I look at the hour") foretells a person's development and destiny based on where the planets were in the sky at the exact moment of birth. A natal astrologist constructs a horoscope chart consisting of one's birth data—the time, place, and date of birth. This horoscope, this diagram of the heavens that shows the relative position of the planets, stars, and sun at the moment of one's birth, can be used to identify talents, strengths, and the most propitious courses one should follow in life, say practitioners. Although most astrologers will not use the word "predict," they surely imply that the heavens *suggest* the general course of a person's character and fortunes.

These choices, however, are not engraved in stone, say most experts. The astrologer can point the way, but the individual is always in control. The heavens show potential, not actuality. The individual makes the choices—not the planets. All anyone can "see" in a horoscope are tendencies that will become facts only if we do nothing to alter them. A favorite saying among astrologers is, "The stars impel—they do not compel."

Today's modern practitioners use computers to compile and interpret all the birth and planetary information at their disposal—taking ten minutes to do what previously involved days of computation. The heavenly patterns in one's personal astrological chart will be studied, factor by factor, and then discussed with the client. Many astrologers also use astrology in one-on-one therapy much as a psychoanalyst uses Freud's writings—as a road map, they say, to a more meaningful and fulfilling way of life.

THE BASIC COMPONENTS OF NATAL ASTROLOGY

• The *sun sign* in a horoscope is the cornerstone, the major tool of a natal chart. It is the constellation of the zodiac that is occupied by the sun at the exact time of an individual's birth. These are the twelve zodiac signs: Aries, Taurus, Gemini, Cancer, Leo, Virgo, Libra, Scorpio, Sagittarius, Capricorn, Aquarius, and Pisces. One's sun sign is said to indicate dominant personality traits—Cancers love water, home, and family, for example; Leos are overconfident, honest, and loyal.

• After the sun sign in importance comes the *rising sign* that is on the horizon at one's moment of birth. Every two hours in every day, a new sign rises on the horizon, sometimes called the *ascendant*. This rising sign marks the differences in character, abilities, and the manner in which one is most comfortable expressing herself among individuals born on the same day but at differing times.

• An astrological horoscope is also divided into twelve equal pie-shaped arcs, and these arcs are called the *houses:* each bears a different influence on one's life. Every possible aspect of one's life is ruled by one of the houses. Although astrologers interpret the significance of the houses differently, basically they consist of personality, finances, communication, early home, children, health and service, marriage, philosophy, profession, friends, and karma.

During a reading many terms will emerge—terms like *transits* (the day-by-day position of the planets as they affect the natal chart) and *aspects* (the flow of force among the planets). Whenever necessary, it's important to stop the reading to ask the astrologer to explain the jargon; otherwise the reading will remain a mystery.

It's pleasant to think of astrology as a new and always developing field, in its infancy, actually, even though it's about five thousand years old. Astrologer Hewitt tells us that the planet Pluto, for example, was discovered only in February 1930.

Who knows what's just beyond the levels of accepted scientific observation?

The Astrologers

MATT LOCASIO

I MEET MATT LOCASIO (NOT HIS REAL NAME) in a hotel room: he's a commuting astrologer who travels regularly from his home state of Wyoming to see his adoring clients in New York, California, Georgia, and Kentucky. Matt's one of a fast-growing breed of paranormal practitioners who counsel as well as practice in their specific genres; he is, in fact, an astrological therapist. Such a practitioner has an edge, say astrology buffs, over plain old psychics because his prescient art also provides clues to the most favorable *time* to make changes. "Astrology helps me better understand the people I'm working with," says actress Angie Dickinson. "It helps me to understand *myself* better," says another believer, "and then I have more ammunition to make important decisions."

Early for our appointment, I sit downstairs in the lobby, feeling a little conspicuous; what if all these business types playing with their laptop computers knew I was waiting to see a strange man in his hotel room for the purpose of reading my stars?

Prior to the session, Matt's sent me a three-page directive that includes general information—his goals, fee, and general structure of the session we will share. I've sent him, also in advance, my astrological dimensions—exact time, date, and place of birth (I've found all this out in advance at the board of health where I've gotten a copy of my birth certificate, listing the details), and he's cast a chart based on these particulars. The positions of the sun, planets, and other heavenly bodies at the precise moment of my birth will have given me certain strengths and weaknesses that have had a direct influence on the way I've lived—and the future choices I should make. What's happening in the skies, says LoCasio, happens over and over again; the universe is coherent and ordered. Astrology, says LoCasio, is a study of heavenly cycles and cosmic happenings as they're repeated and reflected in us, on earth. If only we would look up, we could know everything.

LoCasio's a child of the sixties, with scruffyish long hair, a sweet smile, and a beguiling manner. I didn't ask, but without the benefit of otherworldly insights, I could swear he's been to Woodstock. After some introductory small talk during which I start to feel relaxed, we sit down on the impersonal hotel chairs and he pulls out my natal chart. It certainly looks impressive with its arcane symbols, circles, odd words (Ayanamsha—now what in heck *is* Ayanamsha, and why is she on my chart?), and what appears to be cryptic abbreviations—Fir, Ear, Air, Wat, Car, Fix, Mut.

"Astrology," says LoCasio, "is the perfect science. It is always right. But astrologers are not always right."

A modest beginning. I like that.

LoCasio then tells me, *fast,* that . . . yoursunisinthesignof Libra,yourmoonisinthesignofAquariusandVirgoisrising.

Frankly, this troubles me. In every occupation there is a lingo and a patter that is peculiar to that profession; you walk the walk and talk the talk and sound like an expert. Some people, unaccustomed to asking for explanations, are snowed by this patter; my husband, a lawyer, calls the jargon of his profession "legal beagle bullshit." Matt, to his credit, laughs and slows down when I tell him I haven't understood a word.

People who have their sun in Libra, as I have, says Matt, are "other" oriented: they're relationship oriented because the scales (Libra's sign) represent a desire for balance, for harmony, for finding the common ground.

Well—this may or may not be true of me. Then he tells me that people with their moon in Aquarius have a "level of detachment."

Well, how do people who are relationship oriented (my sun in Libra) also have a level of detachment (my moon in Aquarius)? We're romantics, says Matt, but because both of these planets are *air* signs, we tend to focus on the space between ourselves and others.

Again, I like Matt enormously, but I think this is astrological legal beagle bullshit. Romantics—but we focus on the *space* between ourselves and others? Well, which is it—romantics or space focusers? In a book I've taken out of the library, I've read that Libras make good judges because they can see an issue from all sides, but because they can do this, they have a lot of trouble making up their minds what to wear in the morning. Well, not me—I'm always passionately on *my* side, and you should see me zip through my closet in two minutes flat.

And what about the Virgo rising part? Virgo, says the astrologer, is a sign of critical analysis. LoCasio tells me I'm always looking for what I can do to make things better and fix things. Couple that with Libra's sun, and, says Matt, I have a great sense of self-worth that's been developed by my wanting to get things right.

But, mostly, if you want the embarrassing truth, apart from my writing, I usually just want to get things *done*—not necessarily right. And I'm not such a critical analyzer.

Matt tells me that because Librans are often scientists, writers, or airheads (*airheads?*), they often like to see what effect they're having on other people. "You tend to make others feel comfortable, like Katie Couric," he observes. He says the Libran throws a stone in the water and watches carefully to see the ripples that come back, which can be a plus or a minus: careful observation is good, but the downside is that the Libran can never make up her mind—always watching those ripples.

"There is," Matt notes gravely, "a broad-based personality filter in your chart consisting of four elements—fire, air, earth, and water." He breaks down the elements as follows:

Fire: (representing primitive enthusiasm) = 20 percent. I tend, says Matt, to be an energy miser because I don't feel I have *enough* primitive enthusiasm. *Wrong.*

Earth: (representing practicality) = 10 percent. I'm not very practical and, indeed, even *look* less security oriented to other people. I always march to a different drummer. "Are you married?" asks Matt. "Women with Mars in the twelfth house often are not married because they're connected to a higher ideal." *Very wrong.* (When I tell him, he backtracks and says, "Well—knowing how strong willed you are, it would have to be an excellent marriage to last.")

Air (representing ideas, romance, idealism) = 40 percent. I was very indecisive and procrastinated a lot as a younger person, says Matt. I always needed to be *right,* so I could never submit what wasn't letter perfect. *Wrong.* "The way you learned to materialize your thoughts made you productive," says Matt. I don't know what this means. Neither, it seems, does he.

Water (representing sexuality and connection with others) = 30 percent. Matt says learning to work with groups on shared enterprises is not so easy for me. *A little right.* He says I have a "dismissive" quality, as in "Don't connect me with a schlock enterprise, I'd rather do it myself." *A lot right.*

Matt finishes with a flourish by telling me that mental hospitals are filled with people who are water and air dominated (as I am), and the people are either the patients or the psychiatrists. *That,* I'll buy.

I don't know about astrology. Like my experiences in some of the other genres, it all seems so general: anyone can pick off a piece of the patter and make it fit.

LoCasio tells me that things will keep expanding for me, that the parts of my self that have been most problematic will get more interesting. Being unknown was never going to be sufficient for me, he says. Well, that's true. I *really* wanted to be famous.

He says that in my youth I was very rebellious, but that's tempered now as I've gotten older.

Well, that's wrong. Just the opposite.

He says that the subject matter I've been concentrating on is going to change slightly. I don't give him an A for this, either—although the next astrologer I was to see tells me the same thing. And he says that I'll see subtle changes in the next two years, but a *massive* change in 1998 when Neptune goes into Aquarius.

I'm unimpressed. Who can wait till 1998 to see if he's right? By 1998 I'll forget all about the massive change.

Then LoCasio plays ball.

Your own relationship with your mother, he says, taught you how to mother in her style, but your daughter won't accept that style of mothering.

First base.

The only way she could handle two such powerful, self-assured personalities as you and your mother was to fight back.

Second base.

Your child often felt ignored or controlled by you, but not accepted even though your own perception of your mothering is that you encouraged her to be anything she wanted to be.

Third base.

You're trying to get to a place where you are trying to remove the things that cause her pain because you love her unreservedly, because you miss her.

Home run.

Then there's a lot of stuff about a change in our culture coming—how sexual abuse and financial indiscretions by high officials will pretty much come to an end. I wouldn't give you two cents for that astrological call. Then LoCasio says that the position of Venus and the moon in my chart shows I have an understanding of women and I'm able to communicate with them easily and that that talent will grow. Does the fact that the astrologer knows I write for women's magazines have anything to do with this call, or am I being picky-picky?

Look, this has been enjoyable, but LoCasio's own instructions before the session emphasized that "our time together should assist you in placing the concerns and specific issues of this period of your life into a larger context. Receiving this new information will require some self-stretching. Consequently you may feel overwhelmed by information in your initial appointment."

Not exactly: underwhelmed is more like it. When he did hit it was with intensity, but the rest of the reading felt pretty flat. As I understand it, the heavens can show the parameters involved in my horoscope—my talents and strengths and the possibilities open to me even though my choices prevail and, ultimately, I'm the boss of my life. But what if the information that my horoscope provides is all over the place—I'm a romantic, but I focus on the space between us? My talent will grow, my subject matter will change slightly? Give me a break.

But, to be fair, I need to try this astrology again. It's been around five thousand years: what's wrong with me that I can't see it?

RICK JAROW

So I'm trying again.

I am standing in the entryway of an apartment house in a questionable neighborhood of New York City, ringing Rick Jarow's buzzer (one of his offices is here). Any minute I'm going to get mugged, any minute, any minute . . . What in the world am I doing—risking my *life* to chat with an astrologer—especially when the last experience seemed a fizzle? Here comes, well, definitely, a murdering drug dealer, I know it. *Where is Rick? I am very nervous.*

Finally—the buzzer answers—and the entry door opens. The elevator is not much better, Graffiti Central with a scent of cat pee, and I'm really sorry I came.

When the apartment door answers to my ring, I'm not sorry anymore—in fact, I feel embarrassed for being such a wimp. *People* live here, and Rick, mid-forties, is very tall, very cute, very long haired, very wholesome looking. On the wall of his office is the framed blessing that his great-grandfather wrote out for him at his birth:

> *Hear O Israel, The Lord Is Our God, The Lord Is One. . . .*
> *Blessed Be He . . . the Lord Bless Thee and Keep Thee, the Lord*
> *Make His Face Shine over Thee and Be Gracious unto Thee. . . .*
> *Grandpa Sperling*

Any astrologer who has his grandpa's prayer framed is the astrologer for me. How loony can he be?

Give it a decent chance, Sherry, I repeat to myself. Give it a chance, Ms. Arrogance.

Rick has a Ph.D. in Indian languages and literature from Columbia University, and before he reads my chart for me (as with

Matt LoCasio, I've provided him in advance with my vital birth statistics) we talk a bit.

"Astrology is folklore," Rick says, "a tradition that rises from the soil and the people over millennia. I ascribe to the Jungian point of view, which says that folklore—and thus astrology—expresses the collective unconsciousness of a whole civilization. In some way we can't understand, everything is closely related to everything else regardless of apparent distance or time; something that happens here or happened a century ago can affect something that happens tomorrow."

I am getting excited. I've come to Rick for an astrological consultation, but he has hit upon something I've been working on for a *New Woman* magazine article in another part of my life: *synchronicity*. The word was coined by the very man Rick is talking about, the great Swiss psychiatrist Carl Jung, and it's been defined as coincidences that are so unusual and meaningful, perhaps they can't be attributed to mere chance. Jung believed in an interconnectedness among all things in the universe and that synchronicity—these meaningful "coincidences"—actually linked the material world to the psychic world.

Rick Jarow also believes in links; he's sure that what happened in the heavens at the exact moment of my birth—the location of the planets in relation to each other—can be a blueprint for events that happen to me today and will happen to me tomorrow. Like Jung, he says that everything in the universe is connected—we are connected to the heavens, the stars, the planets, and influences other than the ones we can control. "Your astrological natal chart is a kind of fingerprint or voiceprint that can be read," says Rick. "Astrology can help you find the themes, the deep-base issues, that are really motivating your life.

"And a good astrologer, in a way," he continues, warming to his lecture, "is like a good wine taster, who can take a bottle of wine and tell you where it came from, what kind of a year it was, and what it would taste like in twenty years—just by a sip of the wine. He can do it because he's tasted thousands and thousands of bottles of wine and has developed a kind of sympathy with wine *energy*. A great astrologer," continues Jarow, "after a long while develops a sixth sense of the connections of the planets and their energies and how they configure in a person's life."

So how come, I ask Jarow, for me, those newspaper astrology columns are almost always totally wrong or so general as to be meaningless?

"Because," he says, "they're entertainment, brainless popular astrology that *is* based on generalizations for four billion people. A personal reading depends on three variables: your date of birth—and that's all the popular astrologers ever have—your place of birth, and your exact *time* of birth. Look—popular astrologers are not dopey—they usually know what planets are going through different signs, and they can put an entertaining, engaging spin to it. But there's *no* way it can relate to you because they don't have your other two variables—place and time of birth. Being a Libra or a Sagittarius, by itself, means nothing: it's like saying all people with brown hair will get rich next Tuesday. This is not to say that the popular readings are always incorrect. Every human being is unique, but sometimes, by synchronicity, you can find your true fortune in a fortune cookie or in a magazine horoscope."

I sure hope this reading is better than a fortune cookie.

He begins:

"The rising sign—the sign that was coming over the horizon at the exact moment of your birth—was Virgo. Theoretically, the best of Virgo should give you critical awareness, should make you excel at paying attention to details. The worst of Virgo, though, is not to be able to see the forest for the trees. So, you have a paradox," says Rick, smiling, "and you have to figure out how you're going to handle it—I can't do it for you."

Well, how does my *chart* say I should handle my life? I ask.

"Astrological charts don't advise or predict—they just shine a light. The planets themselves are not controlling—just connecting with us," says Rick. "Astrologers have been known to advise or predict; the charts never do."

I have to think about this some more, but it sounds reasonable.

Rick's on a roll. "The planet Neptune," he continues, "is close to Virgo rising, and that also creates a paradox because Neptune's energy makes you dreamy and Virgo wants things in order. This is another powerful marker for you: you're living a life in which you have to find a balance between reality and idealism."

What Rick says, to be fair, seems to have echoes of LoCasio's reading. As the latter did, Rick also tells me that because I'm a Libra whose sun is "conjunct Venus," I certainly seek balance in most things, am very relationship oriented, and am sensitive to beauty.

What's so special about this reading? I ask Rick. I still don't understand why it's truer than a newspaper horoscope. Doesn't everybody who was born on October 17 have a "sun conjunct Venus"?

"Yes," he agrees. "But not everybody born on October 17 had a sun conjunct Venus *in the second house!*"

Ah—the second house. And Rick tells me about everyone's twelve houses.

"Each house represents the area in life where action takes place. First house is the body, second house is finances, third house is vehicles and communications . . . and it goes on. In each well-drawn horoscope, there are three variables—planets, signs, and houses—and they have to be mixed and matched skillfully.

"Astrology," asserts Rick, "is not a dogma; people don't have to conform to their charts. I may tell you where a strong concentration of energy is, and I will try to point you in the direction of your greatest growth, but what I do not ever say is 'Your chart says you should move to Santa Fe' or 'Don't go to the supermarket on Tuesday' or 'Protect yourself from the horrible time that's coming on the fourth.' "

Here's the deal: Although Rick is saying many of the same things Matt did, I'm relating to him better. I like his way of explaining things to me—never assuming I know the meaning of "conjunct Venus" or all the stuff about houses. I like his intellectual bent, and I don't feel at all manipulated—even when things seem so general as to have little personal applications, and so far, that's been true. It's becoming clear as I research that astrology-made-meaningful depends on the art of the practitioner. Perhaps it's so of all the paranormal genres.

"Virgo risings look younger as they grow older. You bear that out," he tells me with a smile.

Hmmm. That last was kind of nice. Maybe a little *too* artful. Then, bingo.

"There is a square—a challenging aspect between the sun, Neptune, and the planet Sirius," says Rick, "that is *the major* marker in your chart: it has to do with the 'mother' archetype."

Here it is again.

"Your chart," continues Rick, "seems to indicate dramatic life issues involving *mother* and *abandonment;* this could translate into a mother or a child who 'disappears' in a certain sense. It can refer to you and your own mother—her death and 'abandonment' of you; it can refer to you *as* a mother or even you and friends who act as mother-nurturers. I'm not sure what it's all about, but I see the parameters clearly."

But *I* know what it's all about: the issue of mother/daughter in all its complexities, in all the generations of my family, is always a "major marker." What amazes me is that it shows in my natal chart—or else how would he know? Then I think, Well, almost everyone has mother/daughter abandonment issues.

Then I think of four women who don't. This part of the reading would have left them puzzled.

Suddenly I decide to stop looking for the propensities for scam here and just flow with the experience. Think about it later.

Rick tells me a story I've heard before, but today it has new meaning. It's the myth of Persephone, the ancient Greek goddess who is kidnapped from her mother, Demeter. Pluto wants her to be queen of the underworld, so he takes her from her mom. Naturally Demeter is wild with fury at her husband, Zeus, who has allowed his brother Pluto, god of the underworld, to do this; so at first she goes through all the anger of betrayal. In her fury she goes on strike and says, "If you don't give me back my daughter, I'll stop all the plants from growing"—a neat trick, but one that's not just an idle threat, since she's the goddess of corn, harvest, and fruitfulness. But then, says Rick, "Demeter's grief and reason overcome her fury, and as often happens in Greek myths, the gods make a deal: 'Okay,' says Pluto, 'we'll give her back—but not entirely—after all, I've already tricked her into eating that pomegranate that will make her mine.' So the deal is a compromise: Demeter must let her daughter go for part of the year, and then Persephone returns to her mom for the other part—but of her own free will. Seems Persephone *likes* being queen of the underworld—well, for four months a year, anyway.

"I think this myth *is* your chart," says Rick. "It's all about abandonment and loss; we must have our selves dragged down in order to understand our selves most deeply. And I believe," he continues, "that some higher self in us all consciously sets up painful scenarios so we can learn something. The Pluto theme in your chart is about the loss and return of mothers and daughters:

lost ones often return, but not in ways you expect and not by your coercion; they come back, as Persephone did, when you let go. You see," says Rick, "Pluto's role is to give us what we think we don't want by taking away. In the Persephone myth, he takes away Demeter's 'I was the perfect mother, how could this happen' mentality: by dragging her down, Pluto helps Demeter to understand her deepest self—and that of her child.

"In our stage of human evolution," Rick concludes gently, "I believe that humans learn only through crises and by separation and loss."

"Learn what?" I ask, my voice catching; but I'm not embarrassed.

"Well, to quote William Blake," says the astrologer, his blue eyes boring in on me, " 'we are put on earth a little space, That we may learn to bear the beams of love.' I think you're learning new ways to be a daughter—even though your mother has already died—and new ways to be a mother, new ways of caring."

This is heavy stuff—more than I bargained for.

On to other things; the reading takes an hour.

The charts indicate that my life literally will be shaken by the roots in the next two years—starting March 5. This is neither good nor bad but challenging, says the astrologer, and particularly there's a possibility for momentous changes in my family or home situation that will take a lot of energy.

Chiron, the teacher, the shepherd, the healer of the wounded, is in "high focus" in my chart, says Rick. I have to "do battle" with this part of my personality, but essentially, says the astrologer, I tend to be a "reformer"—one who would do well as a teacher or investigative writer with particular appeal to women.

I tell Rick that he didn't have to be a brain surgeon to figure out the writing part since I'd already told him that.

Rick looks at me steadily and says, "I swear I would have said teacher or writer no matter what you told me. I couldn't have said anything else. It's all here." And he points to the chart.

Skeptic that I am, I know he's telling the truth.

I also have to admit that the other astrologer said almost the same thing—and then it seemed silly. Now I'm thinking about it; aside from the obvious "writer" part, Rick's is not altogether a crazy call. I have noticed some "reformer" instincts in my personality. So have friends and other people in my family. It doesn't always make me entirely beloved.

"What's more," he continues, "you have a strong tendency toward victim/savior relationships." When I tell Rick later in the reading that I indeed used to be a teacher—a teacher of cerebral palsied children, he leaps on it and says—"See?—there's the savior part!"

Then Rick stops me short.

"What do you have?" he asks.

What do I have?"

"Quick—answer," he directs, "the first thing that enters your mind: *What do you have?*"

"A sweet and wonderful husband," is what I have.

"Your answer expresses your values," he says, "and since spiritual growth may come through a love of arts, beauty, *or* relationships, your answer shows what values count most to you. And"—Rick smiles—"your answer is absolutely typical of Librans for whom relationship is a powerful value. Although, as the folklore has it, since Libran souls seek the ideal relationship and perfect harmony—they rarely find it, since ideal relationships are not often of this world. You're a lucky Libran."

That's me, a lucky Libran. I'll buy that.

Astrology, says Rick, can be seen as the folklore of civilization. "If you study different astrological systems in different times and places, you will see they clearly reflect the cultural values of the times. A good reading of your astrological chart can give you a very rich vector view, a map of what your life is about that's better, for example, than the Minnesota Personality and Aptitude Test," says Jarow. "Good astrology readings let you know who the gods are that knock on your door. The gods are the energies that erupt within us, our talents, our fears, our innate dispositions. If you understand that the planets represent influences on you, you can better understand the choices you have. And there *are* extraordinary unseen and unfelt influences around you. Look—you can live your life without astrology, but you cannot live your life without listening to the forces around you. Your car has a little rattle—if you don't listen, it becomes a bigger rattle and eventually a breakdown."

I think he's saying that I have to learn to listen to myself. He's also saying that our sense of who we are is so limited that we should dip into whatever disciplines are available to help us break open the mysteries.

"Most of us only listen to the eleven o'clock news as our sole source of information," says Jarow.

"But," he continues, "if we do decide to pay attention to astrology, we really must know that our lives are not predicted in the skies—they're reflected in the skies; what we're looking at in the planets is a mirror of the psyche."

For example, he explains, Saturn with its rings has traditionally been considered a planet that has to do with limitations, holding things in, boundaries. "If someone comes to me and says, 'O wise astrologer, what shall I do with my life in the next six months?' and I see a strong Saturn connection in the person's sun around her, it doesn't mean she's doomed or that she can't get what she wants. It just means that there are energies of containment around her, and she has the choice of how to work with them. It might mean, for example, that this is a better time to save money than spend it, to plan for the future instead of taking a big risk."

One of the challenges for postmodern humanity, notes Jarow, "is to learn to live with different perspectives. No one can claim to have all the truth anymore, not Benetton, not Allan Bloom, not the man in the gray flannel suit. I believe that astrology is one very important perspective to help us find the deep-based themes that motivate our lives. On a more direct level, astrology's also useful for taking a look at your health chart."

My health chart? It shows, says Rick, that my nervous system could be a problem—"you get fried too easily—rattled when you do too much or go too fast." But then he says that I do best as a "multitasker"—doing more than one thing at the same time, something that would shake those who need to concentrate on one thing at a time.

Well—which is it? Fried when I do too much or multitasker proficiency? This reading is starting to sound like the other one: contradictory in its efforts to embrace every possibility.

Rick also tells me that if I were to have a health problem, it would show up in my teeth, bones, inner ear, or back. And, he continues, maybe the stomach.

Not much left, friend. The fact that he's right on two out of five doesn't impress me one bit. I could have done the same for him—without the planets.

Then the astrologer looks serious. "You may have trouble with your Mercury," he says.

"I have a Saab," I answer.

He ignores the pitiful attempt at wit. "You tend to clash with authority figures who may hold you down or create limitations. It makes you want to prove yourself even more. In fact," he continues, "you have a triangle of need. Balancing your need for freedom, your need for a strong relationship, and your need for mother/daughter security is your greatest challenge."

Look, it certainly could be construed as a generality—but it's true.

Happily, he tells me that I'm going to hit my prime in my work in May and all through the spring (which is just when I'm going to be finishing my book). I'm going to do pretty well, financially; there's been some confusion between finances and values since October 6, but I'm moving out of that confusion.

I can't help wondering how the values/money thing will play itself out. Will it be values—or money? I can't wait to find out.

The reading concludes at *exactly* the same moment my tape runs out—just when Rick says, "I will end with telling you that you will soon have a grand opportunity to heal and seal a relationship"—*click* goes the tape, which, by the way, is out of Rick's line of vision. "And *that*," says Rick, smiling, "is a synchronistic exclamation point."

Maybe. I'm getting easier with all this. It's almost as if I've given myself permission to relinquish a little control: I don't have to figure out every dimension of reality. It's actually a relief to think that maybe there *are* influences beyond my consciousness and that if I sometimes make the wrong decision, well, it's not all my fault: the stars did it. *The stars did it, Mom*—are you listening? I am not weak or even less strong if I say there's stuff out there that I don't get—and maybe there are people in here who seem to be better at getting it than I. Well, maybe.

It's cold and windy when I leave, but I walk some dark streets, feeling refreshed, surprisingly unafraid. No one mugs me or even looks at me funny. I feel good. I don't understand why.

Tarot

When Carmen (in the opera of the same name) picked the Death card out of her tarot deck—she just gave up: that's the kind of fatalism many believers in this form of divination share. It was unfortunate for the raven-haired beauty with the rose in her mouth, because wiser tarot players know the cards may be interpreted in many different ways.

Tarot is a divination technique using a collection of seventy-eight pictures presented in the form of a deck of cards. Each picture is a unique symbol, and a tarot reader uses the cards for fortune-telling: the cards "speak to her"—actually yield specific information—and what they say depends on the pattern in which they're laid out.

The seventy-eight-card tarot deck is divided into two parts. The twenty-two most powerful cards in the deck are known as *trumps* or the *major arcana* (meaning "greater secrets"). The fifty-six-card *minor arcana* (meaning "lesser secrets") has four suits of ten cards each: wands (which correspond to clubs in regular playing cards and imply enterprise and distinction), swords (which correspond to spades and imply ill fortune, danger, or strife), cups (which correspond to hearts and imply good fortune and, you guessed it, love), and pentacles (which correspond to diamonds and imply financial and material success). Each suit has one additional court card not contained in regular playing cards, the page.

Each card has a different meaning, and if it is dealt in an upside-down position, it means something else yet again. Traditional tarot cards sport complex and enigmatic pictures, but many tarot readers design their own decks, making them even more beautiful, more scary, or more mysterious—depending on the reader's own idiosyncratic preferences. In some decks even the traditional symbols are altered—for example, birds are sometimes used instead of swords, and the Crone is used instead of the Hermit. In a beautiful tarot deck the look of the cards themselves often sets up a strong reaction in the viewer.

No one knows the origination of tarot. Some say it evolved from the yarrow sticks used in the Chinese I Ching divination system. Some theories link the origin of the cards to Egypt, India, the Gypsy tribes of Romany, and even the legendary island of Atlantis. The known cards date from the Italian Renaissance and were used as a game. No one seemed to use tarot as a divination tool until the mid–eighteenth century, when Antoine Court de Gébelin, a French archaeologist, happened on a deck, proclaimed it to be rife with elaborate fragments of ancient Egyptian lore—and ascribed meanings to each card.

In a personalized tarot reading, the major arcana represent states of being—your mental, emotional, and/or spiritual condition at the time of the reading or the situation being described. The minor arcana describe events or situations. The cards, according to practitioners, give us messages that can be used as tools for gaining insight into ourselves.

The tarot cards are read as the reader goes through a special ritual of shuffling the cards and laying them out in various spreads. The position of each card in each layout holds a specific meaning.

Some practitioners have advised considering the cards as a conversation between two people for the purposes of seeing one's life from new perspectives. Serious tarot experts advise that one not expect definitive advice or hard and fast predictions. For example, they suggest asking not for yes or no answers (similar to the way one uses the I Ching—the venerable Chinese Book of Changes), but for insights that reflect the existing energies within a given situation. Even more problematic for skeptics, though each card and its position has a unique meaning, the entire layout must be looked at as a whole—synergistically—which can influence the individual meanings. All of this will sound pretty vague for non-tarot diehards—but then the Oracle at Delphi was also pretty vague.

Sometimes messages from tarot do seem fuzzy. Occasionally they seem crystal clear and on the nose for accuracy—and that, as with all else, depends on the practitioner's skill. But, sometimes, doing their own tarot readings—and many people learn to do just that—wishful thinkers and would-be psychics project their own fantasies and fears into the meanings of the cards.

Does this prostitute the technique? We have to make up our own minds.

Unlike the cards in bridge or gin rummy, the tarot cards are used in many ways. One psychiatrist commented that a talented professional reader can use the visual symbols of the tarot to bring his patient's subconscious emotions to the surface. Handy, maybe, but hardly paranormal and certainly not divination.

Some people use tarot as a spiritual guide, some for meditation. Tarot reader P. Scott Hollander believes that sometimes, alternative uses do lead to true paranormal insights. "If you give your conscious mind something to do, your naturally clairvoyant unconscious mind can concentrate."

Look at it this way: You go for a tarot reading, but inside you're steaming because you did not get the promotion you expected. You draw a card from the deck—the temperance card, with the picture of a sweet angel looking happily patient. This makes sense, you think, a message to me. Temperance is good; all will come in time. The tarot reader asks you to choose another card, and you draw the offputting Hanged Man, looking very, well, hanged. The reader says the Hanged Man traditionally tells you that personal sacrifice is required to attain your goal. Okay. You've learned something. Could your draw of such relevant cards be more than mere coincidence? Who knows? Have you had a paranormal experience? Probably not.

On the other hand, comedian Steve Martin once did a skit in which he pretended he was the tarot's Hanged Man—just as the noose was tightened around his neck. "If there is a God, give me a sign," choked Martin. "See, I told you that the knulpt smflrt glpptner. . . ."

The Tarot Readers

DEIRDRE

I NEVER LIKED CARDS. Gin rummy bored me to tears, and my lack of bridge-playing ability actually lost me a certain level of college popularity. Once, though, a sorority sister pulled out a pack of tarot cards, and they seemed pretty interesting. She laid them out, facedown, and unaccountably, I remember choosing two cards: one turned out to be an attention-getting picture of two naked people and was called the Lovers. The other card was the Hermit—a seeker kind of a guy with a light. I remember these two cards because secretly I considered myself a little bit of a hermit and certainly, if I ever could get up the nerve to Do It, probably a great lover. I thought it was pretty amazing that I just happened to choose these two; still, I didn't think my sorority sister had psychic abilities. I acted very worldly and made her feel dumb for even having a tarot deck—an endearing trait I had in those days. And tarot went out of my life as inauspiciously as it entered.

So I walk into this office that twenty-one-year-old Deirdre-with-the Map-of-Ireland on her face is borrowing from some executive type so she can give my friend Marshie, a tarot devotee, a reading. I'm only an observer, this time; I figure I'll learn more if it's not always about me.

Deirdre is adorable. She tells me that in Belfast *everyone* does tarot. Reading the cards is a national trait—akin to liking warm beer. I'm prepared to like *her*. She takes out two sets of cards, one wrapped in red silk and one wrapped in purple because . . . well, just because she likes those colors, she says.

She chooses the purple-encased deck and then selects the queen of cups to represent Marshie, who has dark hair and dark eyes, because the queen picture on the tarot card is one of a woman with dark hair and dark eyes. She puts the queen of cups in the center of a Celtic cross—six cards forming the cross and four cards laid in a vertical line to the right.

Hmmm. What happens if you have red hair and green eyes? I think. Is there such a queen in the deck? I also have dark eyes and hair; would the queen of cups represent me, also? Marshie and I are as different as night and day. Don't start, Sherry, I tell myself again. Give it a chance.

Marshie is told to shuffle the cards and choose ten. Then Deirdre starts her litany—one that will be repeated many times during the reading.

"Remember," she cautions my friend earnestly, "the tarot won't tell you what you want to know—just what you need to know."

Sounds fair enough. Deirdre tells Marshie to lay the first card facedown, near the queen of cups. She picks it up—it's the ace of coins. Then she proceeds to tell Marshie that new enterprises are "destined for success," that Marshie should "keep things in perspective," that things may not be goin' exactly as she's planned, and that this may "cause her some anxiety."

The next card Marshie picks is the Empress. A promising figure, I think.

"The Empress," recites Deirdre, "is the Mother Earth card. It says you need to learn to balance your own needs with those of others who use you as a security blanket. It says that practical matters are important and that your initial long-term goals are goin' to crumble, but since every cloud has a silver lining, somethin' better is to come."

"Isn't this, well, sort of *general?*" Marshie ventures, cringing inwardly, I know, at the silver lining comment.

"The cards won't tell you what you want to know, only what you need to know," says Deirdre. Again.

"Well now," she goes on, "I see the intuition card, the ace of wands. Do what your heart tells you to do, not what others tell you. Don't be judgin' others by your standards, and don't let them be judgin' you by theirs. Opportunities are comin' your way," says Deirdre. "I see news of sickness or disappointment—not that it will happen to you," she hastens to add. "Remember, the cards tell you what you need to know, not what you want to know."

I sigh—audibly, I think. And instantly feel guilty. I'm getting this innocent child nervous, this eager tarot reader who hasn't the foggiest idea of what is happening or has happened or will happen to a very complicated Marshie. Deirdre's honest as the day is long—anyone could tell that—and she's trying so hard, but she simply hasn't the foggiest. Marshie's world—sophisticated, traveled, layered—is a zillion light-years from Deirdre's life experience. Deirdre's reading reflects Deirdre's experience—not Marshie's.

Then she says, "Look deeper than the superficial in others; it'll be a real learnin' experience for you. And follow your heart's lesson, be it conscious or subconscious."

That does it for me. For the rest of the reading, which takes another half hour, I sit quietly, but I'm totally tuned out. Anyone who says "be it conscious or subconscious" I'll always tune out. It's the "be it" part.

So much for tarot. There wasn't conscious deception here, but reading the cards is probably not going to work for me.

CASSANDRA SAULTER

Not so fast.

It's not fair to judge an art by one practitioner, says my friend Guy, and he sends me to his tarot reader. I go but plan on tuning out before I even ring the doorbell. Maybe psychics, maybe astrology, but never tarot.

Uh oh! The tarot reader's name is Cassandra. I happen to know that in Greek mythology, Cassandra was a Trojan princess who was given the power of prophecy by Apollo: when she spurned him, Apollo decreed that she was never to be believed. Since Cassandra only prophesied doom anyway, everyone was happy enough to pay her no heed.

I figure this does not bode well for me.

The tarot reader Cassandra (and it's her real name) lives in a tiny apartment on Bank Street in New York's Greenwich Village. She opens the door to me—and she's lovely—a raven-haired, dark-eyed beauty with visible traces of an Italian/Jamaican/French heritage in her bones. She's wearing a marvelous crystal necklace of subtly colored stones and tells me that she's also an artist and often works with these eerily transparent (and, she says, healing) crystals, transforming them into jewelry or mystical keepsakes for certain tarot clients. Since I think healing crystals are a crock, I say nothing.

My back hurts and I'm happy she asks me to sit in a straight-backed chair.

Cassandra works with *four* tarot decks: one of them is a major arcana deck, which she calls Tarot Des Artistes that she's painted herself. It's quite beautiful and hints of the great artists—Picasso, Miro, and van Gogh peek through her own interpretations of the traditional archetypal tarot symbols.

"I developed my own four-deck card layout when I lived in

Italy," she says, "where, incidentally, you need certification to do tarot readings."

Who bestows this certification? On what basis? Cassandra doesn't know. It interests me since many paranormal practitioners tell me they do a fair amount of psychological counseling. And from what I read in the *New York Times,* and in my *Time* and *Newsweek* magazines, it appears that the new frontier of psychotherapy really does seem to be incorporating spirituality. Some sort of certification probably would be in order. But, on second thought, what would be certified—the practitioners' sensitivity? Their *gifts?* How would you do that? When I first heard that the practice of using a reading as psychotherapy had become rather commonplace among spiritual practitioners, it tolled a warning bell: Will they do brain surgery next? But in the United States, to be fair, although paranormal practitioners are not certified or licensed, neither are many of the traditional practitioners who advertise themselves as psychotherapists. Who's to say that wisdom belongs only to those who have passed board exams? Further, the paranormal practitioners assure me that their guidance doesn't involve the dependency one often has on a more traditional counselor. A good practitioner's clients, I'm informed, are permitted to consult for guidance only periodically and never daily or weekly as is the common route in psychotherapy.

Is Cassandra able to intuit what my life is about or what it will become? Or, like Deirdre, will she be so off base, so filled with generalizations, that I'll feel bored rather than amazed? *"Amazed"* is not really the right word. I know it's not fair to look for circus tricks. I just need some proof that there's something else out there that might be personal and specific to *me*—Sherry.

My reading begins. Cassandra tells me that in tarot, the information doesn't really come through the cards but through the energy the client brings to the cards and through the reader's special connection with the cards.

"Five different readers may look at five different cards," she says, "but if the tarot readers are good, the client will get the correct message every time no matter what cards she picks or which readers she sees."

Cut or shuffle each of the four decks, she tells me. While I do that, Cassandra closes her eyes to make a quiet prayer. Am I in the middle of Showtime, I ask myself? PRAYING before a reading?

But, so what. If there's anything to this tarot, I'm not going to get it if I start out with a chip on my shoulder. I like Cassandra, anyway. She seems kind and street smart, less cliché-ridden than the innocent Deirdre. She uses my language, my vernacular. Am I a snob? Was Deirdre doomed to fail in my book because of her naiveté and youth? And then, I summarily reject this hypothesis. It's the result that counts: If Deirdre had predicted a lottery winner for me, I'd have followed her anywhere.

Cassandra lays out the four decks in what seems like a haphazard design and turns two of the cards over.

They're the Hermit and the Lovers.

I say nothing but am inwardly shocked at the synchronicity of the choice echoing my remembered college choices. Cassandra is the THIRD tarot reader who has chosen these cards for me, early on. This may be a coincidence that's too remarkable to be pure chance.

"With this Hermit card, I sense a lot of personal sadness which you hide very well," Cassandra murmurs and turns over another card: the Moon card. "And, this one tells me there's a weight in your center pulling you down: it's about loss. The Hermit with the lantern sometimes signifies temporary withdrawal from others in order for both to get a better perspective. You, who are so used to feeling powerful in situations, have lost all your power in one situation. It sort of dominates this reading," she says, "and frankly, I'm sort of surprised."

"When I did a meditation before you came, as I sometimes do," she explains, "I saw many people asking you questions. People like to talk to you and they feel good when they leave and you bring these qualities to your work. You have both a maternal quality and the talents of an alchemist—you can turn tin into gold—so, I thought this reading would be about your business life."

"But, this Hermit, here . . . are you frightened about losing a loved one who makes you laugh? Have you been too bossy, trying to make decisions for another?"

ME BOSSY? Never.

But, is the universe addressing me? I am going through a beloved person's withdrawal—one who makes me laugh. This Cassandra's not bad; she's sophisticated, she's been around, she's reading *me*. I don't know about the cards. I do dread the loss of loved ones—both real and emotional.

"The Lovers card says you want to change things at work," declares Cassandra.

I love my work—why would I want to change? But maybe, maybe—something different? A children's book? A novel? Nahhh. I'm too scared.

Is anyone in your family a chiropractor, she asks suddenly? No. Do you go to one? No. Well, maybe you should, she gently suggests.

Has she picked up on the gnawing pain in my back?

She turns over the Temperance card. It's appeared twice so far in the reading. The Temperance card, she tells me, indicates that I need patience. "Of course you know you can't do anything about this loss. You need to adjust, to try to correct imbalances. You're seeking the control you're used to having, you don't have it at this point of your life and it's driving you nuts. Patience, my dear."

Tell me about it, Cassandra.

"You can still make magic," soothes Cassandra, "but in a different, slower way—as the feminine side of you would choose as opposed to mowing people down."

Then, she quickly says, "Do you have a connection to Europe—will you be going there soon? I see you doing business there, I see you being spurred by something that you see or something that happens in Italy."

Well, it just so happens that I *am* going to Italy in a few months. And, although I hadn't planned to do any writing there, why not?

The form of the reading changes. Cassandra puts away the three other decks which, she says, give information about me and my place in the world as a whole. Now, she'll use only her own deck: I must ask specific questions.

Hmmmm. I decide to be very careful. I know that unwittingly, I can give information away about myself by my questions. I'll try to be guarded—and ask generalities.

What can you tell me about my children? I ask.

Cassandra sighs at my non-specificity and asks me to again cut the facedown cards and pick ten: she lays them in a Celtic cross.

She turns over the Tower, first. It's a nervous-looking card—a tall, dark edifice with a foreboding clock inscribed on it and a wavy, unsettling rainstorm surrounding it. She doesn't look too thrilled.

Neither am I.

"Look," she says, "the Tower does imply *crisis and it can be* ominous but it doesn't have to be. After a storm comes a clearing. Because your other cards in this layout are so good, they temper your Tower.

"Are you changing the way you're looking at your children?" she asks. The answer is yes—but big deal for that bit of clairvoyance. They're adults now—who wouldn't change the way she looks at grown-up children. It's more than that, though, she says. "You're getting insights that strike and shatter past beliefs—whatever has been rigid before. You have to brace yourself—this may be ego death—the end of *your* ego as far as your kids are concerned—but the beginning of seeing new truths about the way things really are."

All this might sound awfully general to a stranger, but it makes perfect, lucid sense to me. Ego death is what's facing me, damn it.

"It's going to be okay, although it's jarring now," she says. "You're going to change basic relationships. One of your children is making a choice, you hate it. Here's the High Priestess card, that's you—the High Priestess facing away from the tower—who could blame you?"

I'm drawn to a lively card with a picture of a great, golden star on it because it has the number seventeen, my birth date, written on its face. I ask Cassandra about it.

"One of your children who seems also to share a seventeen in some way will follow a star—change a job, make a departure of some sort."

I hold my breath: my son, an attorney, has the same birthday as I and he's just gone into business for himself!

Here's Temperance again, she says: your ability to be the alchemist and add condiments to your son's particular soup is on its way out.

Okay, okay.

"But here, look!" she says with excitement. "Here's the Wheel of Fortune and the Hanged Man together."

I see a guy hanging upside down: frankly, this also doesn't seem to be fabulous news. Do I have to worry about the Hanged Man? I ask the reader. "No," she says. "Sometimes it does mean sacrifice but in this case, it means you look at things from an opposite direction—and that implies creativity. And the Wheel of Fortune implies good Karma. What's happening to you now is a result of what you've wanted and chosen in the past. You and your children have been together in past lives. All of you will find your equilibrium," says Cassandra.

Then, Cassandra cautions me. "Please try to be more specific in your questions."

I cut the cards again. This time, she chooses the cards—so I have no control over them, lays them out in a triangle with one card in the center and turns one over. The Tower again. Arrrgh. Another crisis? Cassandra shrugs.

And, then she turns over a card that really gets me nervous: it reads *Chant de Mort* and Cassandra seems to pass over it fast. Look—I don't think I really believe this stuff but the Death card would give anyone pause. I feel the color draining from my face. Uh, oh! I ask, Why are you going fast over the Death card?

"No, no," she soothes. "The Death card doesn't mean death—it just means change, rebirth, moving away from conditions which cause pain. What's changed is your ability to be the alchemist in your children's life. Perhaps it's time to give up old habits and rigidity to allow for a new life to emerge? Perhaps it's even time, says the Death card, to move to a new stage in your work? A different kind of writing? I think you should try something new with your work—perhaps in Europe. And look, here's the Strength card." Cassandra's hand-painted Strength card shows a woman holding up the universe. I like that. "It's you, Sherry, strong, alive you. In orthodox tarot cards, the Strength card is painted as a woman taming a lion. You will tame your lions, she says. And get your powers back."

Okay. All the same, it's my opinion they shouldn't have a Death card.

I ask a specific question. Is my dead mother present—anywhere?

Cassandra turns up four cards—the Tower (not terrific), the Death card (still don't love it, despite Cassandra's interpretation), the Hermit card, and the Moon card (more heartache?).

Interesting, she says. Interesting? I ask with trepidation.

"Sure—the Hermit is just you missing your mother, you looking for her—nothing more. You look, she's gone—that's all it means. But, I think your mother's still actively influencing you—from where, I don't know, but from *close*. The Tower, Moon, and Death cards? Crisis and heartache—then change in your life because of your mom's death: You're writing this book about a subject you never dreamed of tackling—correct?

Pat, perhaps. But correct.

Then Cassandra asks me to choose four angel cards: they're tiny, white, one-inch rectangles piled up in a painted wooden bowl. Each has an angel etched on its surface. They seem kind of like fortune cookies. I LOVE THEM.

I turn over one card: it reads *Clarity.* The next reads *Transformation.* The third reads *Adventure.* And, the last reads *Trust.*

I'll try to trust—at least, a little more. At least, I don't feel dumb that I've consulted a tarot reader. I don't know whether that's progress or regression.

Maybe I'll do it again, maybe I won't.

Before I leave, Cassandra gives me a gift: it's a celadon-colored, Life Savers shaped aventurine crystal. She puts it on a simple hemp string and I hang it around my neck. It's supposed to guide me through the adventures that the tarot says are sure to come. Look—I don't believe in healing crystals but *aventurine* crystals? I can't wait.

The Gypsy Tea Kettle

But are we to give serious attention to such things?
SHERLOCK HOLMES,
"THE ADVENTURE OF THE SUSSEX VAMPIRE"

HERE, THERE ARE NEITHER GYPSIES NOR TEA.

What happens if you wander in "cold" somewhere, to hear your fortune told? What happens if you trust in fate (not referrals) to bring you a little taste of magic in the night? What do you think happens?

The Gypsy Tea Kettle is up a flight of stairs at the busy intersection of Fifty-sixth Street and Lexington Avenue in New York City: at four-thirty on a fading winter's afternoon, through white lace curtains, one can look down from the Kettle's window and see a Roy Rogers, a Dunkin' Donuts, and an office for chiropractic medicine across the street. Many people consider the readings at the Kettle to be another form of alternative medicine.

The Kettle has been serving its brand of therapy for over sixty years; the fascinating tale of your fortune can be heard in fifteen minutes for eleven dollars plus tips (vigorously encouraged). You can call for an appointment, but most clients just drop in.

I enlist my three college roommates—Sybil, Margie, and Teri—to check out the scene at the Kettle, where you used to be able to get a nice cup of tea and a cookie before you got your leaves read. In the late forties, oppressed with high insurance costs and tight health codes (because it was classified as a restaurant), the Gypsy Tea Kettle dumped the tea and cookies and reconstituted itself as a card-reading (tarot and regular) salon.

I've chosen *three* friends deliberately because I want varied opinions—a sampling of other people's experiences, and this time I also
want to stay on the outside in order to observe impartially. Since
the women are not trained journalists, I've provided each with a
tape recorder so that I may hear what went on in each session.

Not so fast. Tape recorders are not permitted, says the man at
the desk (who's been there for twenty-seven years, he says), and he
won't be swayed. It's the owner's rules, he tells me as he answers an
incessantly ringing telephone:

"Gypsy—how can I help you?"

My hackles rise—this has not happened yet. It's important to
tape so that one can remember accurately; very often what you
think you heard is not what's been said at all. What is the Gypsy
Tea Kettle hiding? Still, I have no choice, and the women will be
permitted to take notes.

Who are the fortune-tellers we'll be seeing? How do you hire
them? I ask.

"You have to take a test," says the man at the front desk.

The room is divided into about eight tiny booths—each big
enough for a reader and a client who sit facing each other over a
small table. The large, clean, front waiting area is decorated with
hanging beads, gold fleur-de-lis-patterned wallpaper, growing
plants, fake Tiffany lamps, and green leatherlike banquettes on
which the eager customers wait their turns. This looks a little like
a doctor's office, actually, with no one really meeting your eyes
and everyone wondering what's wrong with the other—or at least
which of fortune's vagaries brought her to this place for balm.

Who's here? About eight waiting customers of varying ages and
walks of life, including a fiftyish, proud but shabby-looking black
woman; an absolutely gorgeous, blond, Miss America 1996 type;
a chic couple, whispering together—he in a cashmere Armani
coat and muffler, she in Donna Karan, if my fashion eye serves me

correctly; a young, frightened-looking doe of a girl; a Hispanic woman who won't take her eyes off me; and a stunning Jessica Tandy–ish matron, her white hair pulled back in a severe bun, clutching a Bloomingdale's shopping bag. Scraps of conversation filter out to the waiting room from the booths where I can see the fortune-tellers bent earnestly over their cards; one reader is wearing a red plaid shirt and dungarees, another a maroon dress, another a green velvet shift. They look as if they have day jobs in addition to this one—or *wished* they had day jobs. I hear. . .

"Are you worried about it?"

"Has it happened yet? Well, it *will.*"

"He loves you, don't worry."

"The next month looks hard. . . ."

The turnover is enormous. A customer leaves, another fills the vacated booth, another comes in from Fifty-sixth Street. Some must be regulars—at least, they seem to know the routine—and the man at the front desk—who asks Margie, Sybil, and Teri if they want to see anyone special. No? Well, all three can go in now. And they do, each to a different reader. Fifteen minutes pass. All three emerge. We repair to Teri's nearby apartment, and they tell me what happened.

Teri

My reader was from South Africa. She had wonderful red henna hair and bad teeth. She talked a mile a minute. First she asked if I had children. I said no, and she said, "Well, I see a small child. Maybe one of your friends will get pregnant soon." She asked me to pick twenty-one cards, then five more, then five more, and told me what they signified—my health, wealth, fortune. She was not happy with the way I was shuffling the cards—said I could get someone else's fortune if I did it wrong.

When I asked her what the pictures meant, she said it would take too long to explain. "There's a lot of stress in your work," she told me. So what else is new? "It's like a juggling act," she said. "There's a man who will soon be involved in your work, and if it's not a man, it's a very strong woman."

She asked me for the astrological sign of my lover and told me our relationship was good but not perfect. Nothing's perfect, she mentioned. She asked me if I ever traveled with him. I said rarely. She told me we'd take a trip either in four weeks or by April.

You always have a little glimmer of hope that someone who's prescient will tell you something marvelous. It didn't happen. I felt disappointed, even though I should have known better.

Margie

My reader was fortysomething, thin, and small, with wiry salt-and-pepper hair, small eyes, a nice smile. She asked me to cut the cards, then told me I was going to change my job because I was not happy in my present one. Then she asked, "Does that sound right to you?" I'm an actress, I told her, and I love my job, and what you just said doesn't make any sense at all. Then she countered, "Oh, wait a minute—I mean that I see you going out of town with a new part, soon."

She said I'd been in a lot of dysfunctional relationships. That was true. She told me that she saw I had a daughter who was going to get a divorce.

My daughter is happily married.

She said that my son would soon be traveling widely. My son has agoraphobia and never travels anywhere. She said, "What I really meant was that he was traveling away from the womb and separating from you." Smooth. After I told her about the agoraphobia, she told me she sees my son in therapy. Clever.

I felt disappointed. I wanted her to tell me something profound. A younger man would come into my life, she said. He would be innocent and loving and attracted to my independence; he would either be a Scorpio or a Cancer and would have "liquid eyes." She said "liquid eyes" twice.

I wasn't living up to my full potential, she told me, a view shared by my high school gym teacher. When the reader didn't get something right, she'd shrug and say, "Well, sorry—that's what I *see*. It's in the future."

She told me I'd go on a nutrition kick soon and lose some weight so I'd be open for more parts. That didn't sound crazy—I do go on these nutrition binges. She said I've been set free from a twenty-three-year cycle and would go to California and do fund-raising. Fund-raising? You know what? I could get a job doing what she does. And I'd be a better actress.

S y b i l

My reader was matter-of-fact, with short red hair and glasses—maybe in her early sixties. She had a picture of two babies on her desk—I assume they were her grandchildren. As she spoke she picked on her nails, her beautifully polished nails. It was distracting. The whole scene felt shabby. She asked me to cut the deck with my left hand. She was watching me carefully, tuned in, I think, to my nonverbal responses. I was giving her nothing.

Six months ago, she told me, there was a "letdown, jobwise or in a material domain." Is that true? she asked. I told her in a nice way that there had been an *upturn* in my business life. She seemed annoyed. In the new year I would have many changes, she told me, I would make more money and have a new career, but I need to be more positive, and I shouldn't be fearful. No one should be fearful of change, she said, using one cliché after another.

I need to be more grounded, she told me. When I have a disappointment, I tend to retreat. I said, "Don't we all do that?"

"Yes," she said, "but you should look at the *way* you do it."

She had me pick out seven cards. "You'll be happier in four months," she said. "A *major* breakthrough."

Then she asked me to pick four more cards. "I see a strong woman, in your business," she said, "a sister, a friend . . . ?" She waited for me to fill in the space. I didn't.

"You know the power of silence," she said.

I do.

"I see a young man in your business who you should rely on more."

I felt sorry for her. There *are* two young men, I conceded. It was her bailout. "Rely on them more," she said. "Look at them in a new way. Do you have any questions?"

I asked her if she could "do" my husband even though he wasn't there.

"I see a duality," she said. "He needs to be more focused and organized. Time's up—sorry."

You want me to sum this up in less than a paragraph? Is "bullshit" less than a paragraph?

At Teri's house, after we discussed the readings, we sent out for Chinese food. Margie's fortune cookie told her, "Your love life will be happy and harmonious." Sybil's said, "Your mind is creative, original, and alert." Teri's said, "Many receive advice, only the wise profit from it." My fortune cookie said, "Keep an open mind and all will be clear."

They seemed just about as clairvoyant as the tea room fortunes we'd just heard.

Channeling

When it comes to channeling, even the dictionary sounds doubtful. Who could blame it?

The *Random House Dictionary* defines channeling as "the practice of professedly entering a meditative or trancelike state in order to convey messages from a spiritual guide." *"Professedly"* doesn't sound as if Random House believes in channeling.

Other descriptions of channeling from resource sources have not been as kind. Here are some other characterizations: *bogus, amateurish imitation, spurious, phony, ersatz, make-believe, a combination of fraud, irrationalism, and gullibility* . . .

Things flow through channels: water flows through underground channels, wind flows through the channels created by kites, and guidance—religious, spiritual, and practical—is said to flow through people who receive it from entities outside themselves, perhaps angels, spirits, or extraterrestrials on another plane. The "entities," say some researchers, may also be a hidden part of the unconscious mind of the channeler himself.

Channeling, it should be said, is different from trance mediumship. A medium is said to "mimic" the voice of the entity only she or he hears; through a channel, however, anyone listening hears the actual entity—in the flesh or, rather, in the voice.

Like many of the paranormal genres, information given by nonwordly beings to regular folk through an individual whose mind serves as a passageway has been around forever, in many incarnations, in many cultures. As far back as the fourteenth century B.C., in Egypt, Greece, and the Near East, gods like Ishtar, Apollo, Hercules, Zeus, and Amon were invented, and channels, usually priests or priestesses, went into a trance and spoke the words of the god. The early Christian Church considered prophecy through channels to be gifts from the Holy Spirit. In medieval Jewish practice many high rabbis had *maggids*—spirit teachers who spoke to and sometimes through them.

Many noteworthy artists are said to have received their inspiration through channeling. William Butler Yeats, for example, based his mystic work *A Vision* on channeled messages received through his wife, who was a medium. The contemporary poet James Merrill employed messages channeled through a Ouija board into a number of his finest works. The spiritual teachings called "A Course in Miracles" (recently popularized to best-sellerdom by author Marianne Williamson's interpretation) were first dictated by an inner voice to the channel Dr. Helen Schucman, an academic psychologist; incidentally, the inner voice subsequently identified himself as Jesus—much to the embarrassment of Dr. Schucman, who considered herself an atheist.

The practice of channeling has always gone through cycles of acceptance and rejection. Although some groups like the mystical Theosophists remained faithful, the start of this century found channeling pretty much in disfavor, and it wasn't until the late 1960s and early 1970s when interest returned. Then a young writer named Jane Roberts, trying to develop her ESP ability, made contact with an entity named "Seth," who first communicated via the Ouija board, then through mental messages, and finally through his possession of Jane's body. Through her *Seth* books, Roberts made the channeling of higher entities (rather than spirits of the dead) extremely popular.

Then, in the New Age of the 1980s, we read about the experiences of a woman named J. Z. Knight, who supposedly channels a 35,000-year-old warrior king's spirit named Ramtha. Although Ramtha got some uneven press after he advised individuals to buy J. Z. Knight's Arabian horses, he's still pretty popular. Ask actress

Linda Evans (she *looks* like a reasonable person), who thinks that "Ramtha helped me find happiness. For me, he's been a powerful teacher." Ask actors Ted Danson, Michael York, Lesley Ann Warren, Barry Manilow, and Sharon Gless about Lazaris, the entity who's taken over the body of Palm Beach channel Jack Pursel; they'll tell you how grateful they are to Lazaris (whom Gless thanked when she accepted her Emmy).

Actress Shirley MacLaine wrote about her experiences with California channeler Kevin Ryerson in her best-selling books *Out on a Limb* and *Dancing in the Light;* that really put channeling on the lips of Middle America.

One of the most intelligent books written on channeling is *With the Tongues of Men and Angels,* by Arthur Hastings, Ph.D., a professor at the Institute of Transpersonal Psychology in Menlo Park, California. Hastings, whose basic interest is in communication, writes with humor, knowledge, and practicality about channeling as a higher form of communication. He offers these five basic elements that channeling must encompass if it is even to be considered a "real thing":

1. *The message should be coherent and intelligible.* This precludes receiving of unknown languages in any form. One woman, relates Hastings, says she channeled the spirits of dolphins who go "boop, boop, queep, toot." Such a message would not meet an acceptable Hastings standard.

2. *The source must be perceived as coming from outside the conscious self.* In other words, says Hastings, the channel must not be making it up—either consciously or unconsciously. One interesting way to check this: Note if the information and ideas given are beyond the knowledge of the person doing the channeling. For example, if the channel begins speaking in a secret language that you and your recently deceased best friend *made up* and

never told anyone else—that's pretty good evidence, wouldn't you think?

3. *The origin of the message is perceived or identified as a definite source.* You know who's sending it. In other words, messages that come from "intuition" or "creativity" don't count as channeled messages.

4. *There is an audience for the channeled message.* The message has to be directed to a person or people and not a generalized, amorphous concept.

5. *Finally, the channeled message must have a purpose, which may be to inform, persuade, evoke feelings, or inspire.*

Hastings, who studied dozens of channels, was himself "deeply impressed" with the psychic quality of his subjects' advice. "I'm convinced that few of them are faking," he says. "But whether the entity is a part of their own unconscious, similar to a multiple personality, or whether they connect in some way with a vast pool of knowledge stored in another dimension, I don't know."

I don't know, either.

But here's the consensus of opinion on channeling: It's a mixed bag. Charles Tart, author of *Open Mind, Discriminating Mind,* says that although "not one high-minded entity has ever come up with a carburetor design that would improve gas mileage . . . much of what they say is good common sense. Its attribution to an exotic source makes us more likely to pay attention."

That's where it is for many of us. Many of the channelers seem to be wise people, at the very least. Even if you look at your channeling experience as little more than a science-fiction adventure, the advice and answers the channelers provide are usually thought provoking and, in a very strange sense, comforting.

Hastings, speaking of the values of "justice, wisdom, righteousness, humility, compassion, service, knowledge, self-respect, understanding, and love," concludes his book by saying, "Whether the tongues of channeling are from the minds of men and women or from the angels, their messages often remind us of those values. We should take these messages seriously, so that the knowledge that comes to us from channeling, or any source, will be used in wisdom and love for the benefit of people and the world."

Boop, boop, queep, toot.

The Channeler

CLAUDIA CUSSON/MCDERMOTT

GET CHANNELED? The only one I ever heard of who did it was actress Shirley MacLaine; it brought her best-selling books, but also a lot of bad jokes. Channeling is truly something I never thought I'd experience. But it was my next adventure.

Hardly expecting to hear back, I called Shirley MacLaine's office to get a recommendation from her—but, return my call, she did—a generous gesture, considering the wackos who must barrage her mailbox. MacLaine suggested I contact her personal channeler, "the best, the *best!*"—a Kevin Ryerson in California—but a trip west was not practical for me at the moment. Still, I did want a channeler who came highly endorsed, having learned that in the business of the paranormal, the name of the game is personal recommendations.

A friend of a friend suggested Claudia Cusson in Vermont, who could channel over the phone! Perfect.

Perfect? I reconsidered. Channel over the telephone? How possible is it that someone would be able to access information from her own private spirit, who would then contact *my* own private spirit to obtain multidimensional knowledge directly affecting me—even as I held on to our mutual AT&T link?

Then I felt really dumb. If it was possible that anyone could do this *at all*—why not over the telephone? Why not even over a toy telephone? Why not over a celery? Such a higher being would not be daunted by a small thing like the distance of a few hundred miles, when it was reporting from the vantage point of a few thousand years.

Claudia sent me a form letter confirming the time and date of our appointment. Part of it read:

I work with a spiritual guide whose name is McDermott. . . . The information that will be shared during the session will come from your own spiritual guides. McDermott will attune to them and then share with you what they understand about your growth, life, healing, and spiritual process. I basically function as a translator of the information from your guides and higher self.

I am asked how I can receive this information over the telephone. The channeling process works through attunement, which knows no boundaries. Through this alignment we are connected through wavelengths which are able to be received by myself and the guides. There is probably a more technical explanation, but I simply know there is no difference for me working over the telephone or in person.

At the specified time I called Claudia, who prepared me by explaining how, when the session started, I would first hear her voice welcome the guides and then I would hear her voice change when she tuned into McDermott. During the first five or ten minutes I was just to listen to the guides speak through Claudia; McDermott would be listening to my guide, and with Claudia acting as a kind of translator, all would then talk to me.

Before we begin, I ask the channel *how* she actually gets her information from McDermott—was it through words or visual images? She answers that it is like "seeing/sensing/knowing all at once. I'm not seeing visions as in a dream, but I'm 'seeing' an impression with an associated feeling that I understand. It's kind of like watching a mime: I interpret it as I go along. The guide will close the session when it's time, and you can either hang up or wait for me to come back on the line for a few moments," she concludes.

Ready to start. But wait another minute! I ask Claudia to tell me what she looks like before we begin, because I'll be happier if I have a visual image of her—as a channel. She tells me she's forty-six years old, five feet seven, about 118 pounds, with longish brown hair and a combination heritage of Irish, French, and Native American, covering, it appears, all bases. She will channel with her eyes closed, and "I've been told I do a funny thing with my foot, as I work; I think McDermott has a bad leg."

Okay, now we're ready.

In Claudia's voice:

Masters and guides, we welcome you forward into our circle and ask you as you come forward to sit with us that you may bring wisdom and clarity, balance, alignment, and protection. We ask also that only the highest, most aligned energies be represented, that any and all not in harmony be given what they need in the light. We offer up heart to the masters in healing so that they may amplify and use it to help any and all who are reaching out. We ask as well that our own guides and masters in their world be given what they need to progress so that in their progression they will be able to touch back upon us; we ask that heads of state, powers of all nations, people of all worlds, come forward into their hearts. We ask this always in the highest consciousness as we welcome, await, and turn the power over to you, the masters.

The sound of heavy, deep breaths comes over the telephone. More very deep breathing. A serious breather. If I didn't know better . . . But then I stop myself: why do I have to make a mental joke out of everything—to forestall being shocked by the unknown? In a somewhat higher but more self-assured voice with a slight East Indian accent (the voice pronounces "pat-*tern*" with a prominent *t*), McDermott, through Claudia, says:

Greetings to you, dear friend, from your time, from your plane, from your world, and from your level of consciousness; now, you're in a very suspended pat-tern, and I want to describe to you what that means. . . .

McDermott/Claudia tells me that in another incarnation, about five hundred years before the birth of Christ ("you're an old soul"), I was one of a royal family who "was apart from the masses of people," but I learned discipline in that lifetime because my "heart was bonded to the people." Many of my personal qualities of compassion and creativity were developed in that time, reports McDermott, in the region of what is now the Central and South American countries during a period of history that is just now being discovered. Now, he informs me, my goal in *this* era is to be in a place of service and empowerment—a place I also was in as royalty—but this time "walking with the people, not apart from them, because the true masters have always walked with the people."

Okay. I'll buy that. Royalty? I like it.

The guides (through Claudia) then tell me that my father (who is alive) is very close, almost attached to me, and over the next few years I will be trying to separate myself from all I believe him to be.

Actually I don't mention it, but I've never been close to my father and thus have never had a problem separating from him—even though I've been responsible for his care ever since I've been an adult. This bit of misinformation serves to make me very wary; I don't know about this channeling. But then McDermott says that my mother's mother and my mother had dense fears that I seem to have inherited. Getting warmer.

Then the guides get really hot. There is something, reports McDermott, that is "incomplete" about my mother's burial.

No, I respond, she died over a year ago, and the burial is definitely complete. No, it isn't, says the guide, there's something in the "condition" of the burial that's incomplete, and it's irritating my mom, more than a little.

Then it hits me. I *have* been feeling a little guilty because I haven't yet ordered what the cemetery officials call "perpetual care," which is the planting of greens on my mom's grave; whenever I visit, I can almost hear my mother's voice criticizing me, "Sherry—people come and the place is a mess!" She does seem cranky about it. It's exactly the kind of thing that would make her cranky.

Could the barren grave be what's "incomplete"? I ask McDermott/Claudia/my own guides. No doubt about it, they answer.

(Later I recount this part of the experience to my friend Carol, who's asked me if I've found my mom. I don't know, I'm not sure, I answer her. Incredulous, she snaps, "Well, damn it, Sherry, tell me, please, just what *would* it take for you to be sure?")

Through the Claudia channel I hear many more things—actually, forty-five minutes more on how to attain a higher spiritual self and how to achieve greater balance for this and future lifetimes. Much of what I hear has to do with my concept of "responsibility" and how it is a recurrent pattern in my ancestry. It appears that I've worked on my personal blueprint on this issue of responsibility through many "karmas."

My perpetual problem, say the guides, is that I eternally feel I have to take responsibility for others—those I love—like my children, my husband, and my parents and even those I don't love so much. In doing so, I take away their right to choose what they need for themselves. The highest definition of responsibility, say the spirit guides, is *to respond*—not *to be responsible for*. But it appears that my understanding of responsibility for aeons has never been in perfect balance because I need to put myself in charge of others' expression. Wrong, says McDermott/Claudia: each person must have her own choice of response, whether she chooses to respond with joy or suffering; even if my mom chose suffering, say the spirit guides, her soul needed the experience, and because it was her choice, she's at peace. But when I take charge, say the spirits, assume responsibility for others, make their decisions for them, I deny their expression. I see my family as something of mine instead of knowing in my heart that they're divine and eternal and empowered with the light of their own teaching. My definition of love creates compression, says McDermott/Claudia, when love needs expansion.

I *take responsibility for*, say the guides, because I fear for others. But the real truth about love is divine acceptance of the path others choose to walk. The spirit guides, through Claudia, say the following:

Taking responsibility for others is to support weakness, and it will eventually make you angry at yourself and angry at those who couldn't teach you to do otherwise. Your higher self will evolve when you really understand this. In fact, try to shift your patterns even though others may look at you squirrely when you first start to do so. When you feel a burden of responsibility give it back to whom it belongs. Say, "Thank you, but I'm giving this back because I honor you, and here is your freedom."

The spirit guides ask if I have any questions.

Yes, I do. Is there a special aspect that I should be writing about? I ask, sensing that the session is drawing to a close.

The answer is instantaneous. Write about this—about responsibility, say Claudia/McDermott/my own guides.

What's been said is not untrue. I *do* have, I guess, an unappealing habit of taking responsibility for others when I worry that bad things will happen to them if I don't. My mother did the same thing. I don't know what my grandmother did—but I have my suspicions. If the truth be told, though, I hate my need to feel responsible for everyone. It makes me feel put upon.

I want to learn to *respond*—not *be responsible for.*

Now, here's the thing: I think about what's happened here for many days after it's over. It *occupies* my mind. Some of it has been quite general, and some has been wrong.

But what the spirits said about my dad—was it really wrong? Couldn't I look at it metaphorically—that I've been "close" to him because I felt too responsible for him, not because I felt happily connected?

Do I believe that Claudia Cusson really channeled another entity who gave her all these wise words about me?

Oh, God—I don't know. If pressed, I'd have to say that I don't really think so.

But why not? I do know this. Something is out there, something in the world that can't be rationally explained. Something there is in me also, that says I'm a fool if I don't hear the "something," if I don't believe—*at least a little*—in the unbelievable.

What's definite: these weird happenings, true or not, have caused me to look inward, be mindful, think harder than I ever have about the way I conduct my life and the choices I make. They are better than a year on an analyst's couch.

For example, I am working hard lately on *remembering* accurately—and the channeling experience seems relevant. Thinking about responsibility pulls me back into memories of how I treated responsibility in the past—and how I treat it today. I think this is the first time in ages I've been clear on what happened during the years of my growing up and young adulthood, and that clarity's helping me change my present patterns.

I'm part of the generation that automatically blames its parents for everything bad that happens. Up until this channeling thing, it's always been my mother's fault that I wasn't brave enough to go to medical school but became a teacher because she thought it was an easier and "safe" alternative. Further, it's always been her fault that I was manipulative with my own children—wasn't *she* manipulative with me, and wasn't she my inescapable role model? And it's certainly my dad's fault that I always came to him to start my compositions for school. Why did he allow me to depend on him (and, later, other sources) for ideas? Listen, it's *still* his fault I have trouble writing fiction, which requires me to come up with stories I have to invent. He ruined me forever. My memory tells me so.

But wasn't it *also* my mom who told me I could do anything I wanted? And wasn't it I who chose her (and her fear of risk taking) as a role model for motherhood when, as a grown-up, I could have chosen anyone I thought was smarter to emulate? And (remember carefully, Sherry!) wasn't it really I who, looking as scared and incapable as I could manage, cajoled my dad into starting my compositions? I didn't *have* to use his leads; even a child can choose the easier way—or the responsible way. I chose to take as my own, my mom's style and my dad's inventiveness. I didn't have to.

It's important to get memories right. One travels backward—how many years, how many centuries?—to discover how one moved forward, and if one's memories are gilded or perverted—our courses are thrown off. It's hard.

"I tell the future," said the fortune-teller in Thornton Wilder's *The Skin of Our Teeth*. "Nothing easier. Everybody's future is in their face. Nothing easier. But who can tell your past, eh? Nobody!"

Up until this channeling thing I've been dead certain of my memories and my past, certain that responsibility and choosing for others was thrust on an unwilling me. Suddenly I'm not so sure; could it be that I seized that particular power? Up until this research I've considered myself a skeptic. Why, then, am I surprisingly open to hearing the voices of the unknown? Maybe it is simply a childish longing for guidance and purpose in what sometimes seems like a sea of randomness.

But maybe my new reflective practices are some sort of gained practical wisdom. After all, haven't I always had contempt for dreary souls/scientists/professors who bow only at the throne of Reason, who feel themselves exempt from silliness, folly, love, in unexpected places—and from the wisdom of spirits who may remember better than they?

Do I believe, then, in my spirits from the past? The question keeps haunting me. How come I can't just say no?

Heavy breathing over the telephone.

"In the living truth and the living proof, you will know who you are," says McDermott. "Good day. . . ."

"I'm back," Claudia announces.

Well, just in case, I'm dying to know: Did I have more than one spirit guide, and did they, like McDermott, have names?

I think I saw two or three guides, Claudia-the-channel answers softly, and I can't be sure, but I think they like the letter *J*: maybe one of them was named Joshua or Jeremiah or even Jeronimo.

Geronimo with a J? Why not. Anything's possible.

Boy, this trip is some ride.

Numerology

The god delights in an odd number
VIRGIL

Numbers don't lie. If you believe in numerology, you believe that.

Numerology is a form of divination that operates on the premise that the universe is formed in a mathematical pattern; all things, according to the system, have a supernatural meaning or influence that can be interpreted or expressed by *numbers*. By reducing birth dates, names, and birth places to numbers, it's possible to create a personal chart that is a blueprint of *you*—who you are, the tools you have to work with, and your destiny—as well as a mapping of your soul evolvement—according to Wisconsin numerologist Ken Nelson.

By reducing words and dreams to numbers, you can even predict the best paths to follow. Numerologists, for example, are consulted as children are named, careers are pondered, and businesses are created.

Pythagoras, the pre-Socratic Greek philosopher who lived in 582 B.C., is thought to be the father of numerology, and his followers believed that, beginning with the discovery of the numerical relations among musical notes, the essence of all things was number and that all relationships—even abstract concepts like justice—could be expressed numerically.

Although numerologists differ in their readings, all believe that each primary number is ascribed certain characteristics and values. Some even think numbers have a male or female aspect, odd numbers being masculine, active, and creative and even numbers being feminine and passive—clearly a prefeminist concept. The Greeks and Hebrews considered 10 the perfect number, and Pythagoras himself said that 10 is the essence of all harmonic and arithmetic proportions and, like God, is tireless.

The theory that numbers are energy patterns of vibrations became popular in the nineteenth century when light, magnetism, and electricity were new and fabulous scientific discoveries. Numerologists believe that one's full given birth name is the total expression of the vibratory forces of the universe—and, reduced to numbers, that name will determine one's character and destiny. What happens if your name changes—if you adopt a pen name, for example, or if a woman takes her husband's name? According to experts, the factors of character and destiny can be altered—sometimes negatively—but after several years the vibrational patterns can readjust to the change.

The Numerologist

KEN NELSON

HERE'S HOW IT WORKS, says genial numerologist Ken Nelson, a much sought after Wisconsin practitioner who makes a pretty decent living counseling individuals and businesses on the possibilities inherent in their numbers.

Numerology reduces all numbers to nine roots between 1 and 9, says Ken. Each of the nine numbers corresponds to a letter of the alphabet. To find your "numbers," write numbers 1 to 9 and underneath write out the alphabet like this:

1	2	3	4	5	6	7	8	9
A	B	C	D	E	F	G	H	I
J	K	L	M	N	O	P	Q	R
S	T	U	V	W	X	Y	Z	

To find the numerical value of your name, add together the numbers of each letter; then reduce the numbers to a single digit by adding the total together. For example: my birth name is Sherry Judith Suib.

S = 1	J = 1	S = 1
H = 8	U = 3	U = 3
E = 5	D = 4	I = 9
R = 9	I = 9	B = 2
R = 9	T = 2	
Y = 7	H = 8	

Added together, these numbers come to 81.

$$8 + 1 = 9$$

The numerical value of my name is 9. That is sometimes called the *total expression,* notes Nelson.

Numbers like 11, 22, 33, 44, etc., are considered *master* numbers and should not be reduced to single digits. If your name corresponds to these numbers, you are said to be a highly spiritually evolved person.

We can go further and further with comprehensive name analysis. Every number has an energy of its own, says Ken Nelson. For example, he notes:

1 = independence, creativity, individuality

2 = cooperation, duality, patience, understanding

3 = sociability, a love of learning

4 = organization, logic, practicality, a love of nature

5 = change, impulsivity, pleasure, sensuality

6 = harmony seeking, perfectionist, balance, responsibility

7 = religiosity, mysticism, honesty, psychic ability

8 = power, business success, efficiency

9 = universal understanding, service to others, mental achievement

Be sure that all these number energies, says Nelson, can be used either positively or negatively—depending on the individual's choices. For example, if your name equates to a number 7, you can use your energies for dishonesty instead of honesty.

And we can go even further:

The numerologist says that one can find his or her *soul urge* by adding up the numerical equivalent of the vowels in a birth name.

Or one can find the *life path* or general direction of a life by finding the sum of the month, day, and year of one's birth. Some numerologists, like Nelson, add just the day of birth to find the single-digit number that will express the life path: I, for example, was born on the seventeenth of the month, so my life path is 1 + 7, or 8. (I even have another 8 in my name—the *h* in Judith).

One can find the aspects of *personality* by adding up the consonants.

The sum of one's full birth name *and* birth date is a *power* number, which acts as a lifetime guide or beacon.

The *frequency* of various letters (numbers) indicate the karmic lessons one will face in life.

The *inclusion table* is also important in one's numerological chart, says Nelson, and this indicates the numbers that are missing in one's name analysis and what their absence signifies about one's past and future. In my birth name, for example, there's no sign of a 6 anywhere! Not a single 6.

All words can be converted to numbers to determine how decisions can clash or complement one's life—including one's choice of career, place of residence, and the best day to leave for Istanbul. Some people use numerology to decorate their homes in much the same manner as the Chinese use the concept of feng shui to place their furniture in harmony with the gods and life forces.

An experienced numerologist can takes days to draw up a complete chart based on the various numbers of your birth name and birth date. It is a technical masterpiece, but utterly incomprehensible until explained. Nelson drew my chart and sent it to me with an accompanying tape so that I might hear his interpretation as I followed along on the paper. Here are some of the aspects of my chart; using the numerical formulas explained earlier in this section, you can transpose my numbers to yours—and see your destiny.

Numerology Reading for Sherry Judith Suib. Since my name is heavy in nines (the numerical value of the added-up letters, not to mention the two *r*'s in Sherry and the *i* in Judith—also nines), if I used my vibratory energies positively, my life should be rich in universal understanding, service to others, and mental achievement.

My *life path* (the sum of the day of my birth—1 + 7) is an 8, representing power, business success, and efficiency—all of which are indeed very important to me.

My *destiny*—the combination of my (8) life path and my (9) total expression—equals a 17; 1 + 7 is also an 8 destiny. It looks as though my life path and my destiny correspond nicely.

The first letters of names, says Nelson, indicate one's mental approach to situations. The *S* (a 1 numerical value) that begins "Sherry" tells Ken I am driven to be individualistic and creative. The *J,* which is the first letter of "Judith" (also a 1 value), accentuates this. Ditto the *S* that is the first letter of Suib.

He's got me coming and going.

My missing sixes—that of the *inclusion table*—tells Ken that in earlier years I may have had some misunderstandings of where my *responsibility* lay and that may have had something to do with my "father situation." The sixes, says Ken, deal also with the balance of dealing with others—the forgiveness of and respect for self first, before forgiveness of and respect for others.

Note: This comment knocked me out. Too many other paranormal practitioners have commented on my issues with responsibility; it's a weird coincidence.

Generally speaking, my numbers told Ken that I have a student's need (the two *u*'s in my name) always to learn new things—but that I should go with my intuitive self, my gut feelings. First I thought this was a contradiction—but maybe it's not. The *y* in my name shows a touch of Greta Garbo—I need *alone* time, self-searching, meditative moments—*but* my 8 "path" shows I like best to be around people I can dominate. I look for fame and kudos, and I have strong materialistic drives—*but* my 9 "soul urge" and my 9 "pinnacle" says that my focus in life is to serve others and give them advice, which is very appreciated and makes me good to be around (tell that to my children).

The reading on the tape went on for over an hour, with every possible numerical configuration discussed. It got a little boring—even though commentary on yourself is generally pretty fascinating. Ken figured out that my pen name—Sherry Suib Cohen—is also rife with eights and nines, which proves "that we never stray too far from the well."

Ken Nelson is a compassionate, shrewd reader. He made some errors. He said, for example, that my challenge all through life is to learn how to be alone. Well, that's an inaccurate call: I spend most of my time happily alone.

Still, to my surprise, he was more right than wrong.

Being lousy in math, I've always considered numbers my enemy. Perhaps now they're still something less than best friends, but I no longer fear them.

Numerology, says Nelson, "is the most honest, fast, detailed, and accurate of all sciences: numbers hold the answers to the mysteries of the God force and the universe." Maybe.

Maybe not.

The Tea Leaf Reader

If pigs grow restless and grunt loudly and if they jerk up their heads, there will be a great deal of wind. If a pig picks up a piece of wood in its mouth, it's a sure sign of bad weather.
FROM "SECRETS OF GYPSY FORTUNETELLING"

I'M IN SAN DIEGO, CALIFORNIA, and my friend Matt, a public relations guru, takes me to his favorite hangout, a tea leaf reading room in a moderately fancy condominium apartment complex. Matt assures me that the rest of the apartment owners don't know a Gypsy fortune-telling business is operating from here.

"People come in discreetly and leave quietly," he says. "Why is it different from any tenant who just happens to have a lot of guests?"

Matt's about to have his leaves read—something he does with the change of seasons—and I ask if I can watch.

There's no sign on the apartment door—just a friendly Christmas wreath. We ring the bell, and a woman answers and embraces Matt.

I don't believe this.

If ever there was a cliché, this woman is it. She's got on what seems like at least four layers of colorfully printed skirts, each in a different print; a scarf around her head matches none of the skirts. Her hair is ink black, she has a prominent beauty mark on her left cheekbone, and when she smiles, no left canine tooth. This woman comes from Gypsy Central Casting. Does she look like this when she leaves her apartment to go grocery shopping, or does she transmogrify into someone's mom with a shopping cart?

Matt introduces us. Kathy is her name. If ever there was a Kathy who didn't look like a Kathy—we've got one here.

She waves us to a small round table, and I watch.

First she takes down a small box and a pure white—and, I might add, very clean—cup from a shelf above the table. She opens the box and shakes what looks to be about a spoonful of dried mint tea leaves into the cup. She rises and goes into what must be the kitchen, because she returns in a moment with a steaming red enamel teakettle and fills the cup with water. It can't be boiling because Matt picks it up—and drinks almost all of it, in three swallows. Kathy explains that Matt is energizing the leaves with his soul (which apparently leaks out of his mouth). Then these are the things that happen.

Kathy asks Matt to hold the cup in his left hand by its handle and turn it around three times, clockwise. He does, making a peculiar swirling motion, the effect of which is that the teaspoon of water that's left sloshes out and the soggy leaves seem to stick everywhere along the sides of the cup. Kathy neatly whisks away the spilled water with a small square of what used to be a Turkish towel—which she then places on the saucer.

Kathy tells Matt to turn the cup over and place it on top of the towel on the saucer, then place his right hand over the upturned cup. More energy? I ask her. She nods yes but doesn't look happy at having the ceremony interrupted with a dumb question.

Matt looks a little sheepish.

Kathy rights the cup. I notice some leaves are lost, left on the towel. I call this to her attention. She nods, says it doesn't matter.

The moment has arrived. It's time for the reading.

Kathy stares hard at the cup, turns it several times, checks it out from many angles. She squints. Then she becomes irrationally excited. Look, look, she says to Matt—here's the pail. I look closely at the leaves to which she points. Well, maybe there is a kind of pail shape there.

I knew it, he says glumly.

The pail means, says Kathy, that one should bail out of a bad situation immediately: things will not get better.

But then she brightens. There's the rocking chair! she exults.

The rocking chair, she says, is a sign of a long life.

I can't see a rocking chair where she's pointing. But apparently Matt can. And he's pleased.

And the roof, she says.

I can make out a roof. But it could be a shelf. Or a plate. A roof is protection and security. Probably money coming, says Kathy.

Then she warns: Here's the knife. Someone's out to harm you, she mutters, and with the blade pointed *to* the handle, it means false friends.

Both look at me suspiciously. I try not to look false.

It goes on like this. Sometimes I can make out the symbol she points out, more often not. A ring could mean marriage, soon: doubtful, in Matt's case. A wolf warns of jealous intrigues in Matt's future. Finally Kathy points to a glob, just a glob.

The lion, she announces. Your leadership will be recognized. You will reign supreme during the next two months.

Matt grins.

Now, says Kathy. The question. You have only one. You know.

Matt asks the cup a question. First he writes it on a piece of paper, then he holds the paper over the cup. Then he reads it out loud.

Will I get the Florida account? he asks.

Yes, says Kathy, peering deep into the cup.

On the way down in the elevator I say to Matt, "You've got to be kidding."

"It can't hurt," he says with a grin.

So?

So where am I with these double messages all over the place? Where have I gotten looking for me? For every charlatan like Kathy, I've met a fascinating practitioner like Rick Jarow or Claudia Cusson, who seems to be operating with real talents *I* sure don't own. For every true thing I've learned to trust—such as the way I *know* how growing tomatoes will smell or the comfort I *know* I'll feel in my husband's arms—there are other truths and those who have their own, different ways of *knowing* things, and I can't for the life of me understand how they do it.

The Wisest Scholars

Perhaps some people can communicate with unseen entities or without using speech, hearing, smell, touch, and sight—but most of us just don't know how to do it yet. Perhaps we all have an underdeveloped supersense that can let us send messages to each other through only our minds; perhaps we can all learn to "see" objects, people, or events that are happening far away or even events that will happen in the future or have happened in the past; perhaps, hidden deep in our psyches, is the power of mind over matter—the ability, for example, to move objects or heal people or bend metal simply by using the mind in a certain way. Perhaps we can make remarkable coincidences, even miracles, happen. Perhaps.

In their extraordinary book, *Margins of Reality,* Robert J. Jahn, a professor of aerospace sciences and dean emeritus of the School of Engineering and Applied Science at Princeton University (no flaky campus, that), and Brenda J. Dunne, manager of the Princeton Engineering Anomalies Research Laboratory, tell the story of the king who directed the wisest scholars in the land to prepare the quintessential statement on the nature of reality.

It took many years, but the savants finally produced an enormous, a *humongous,* body of work describing the nature of reality. Not good enough: the king told them to get it down to just one paragraph. Years later, after excruciating debate, the scholars finally presented the one-paragraph result to the ungrateful, cranky king, who further instructed them to boil down their research to just one word. *One word?* Yes. They had to try.

For the rest of their lives they labored, these wise people, these scientists, these scholars—many dying in the search for the ultimate truth: What is the nature of reality? Finally, near death themselves, the few surviving wise men shuffled forward to present to the aged king one crumpled, deeply erased parchment on which was written only one word, as per the king's direction:

PERHAPS

Perhaps looking for me is an exercise in *perhaps.*

Part III | Looking for More

Spengler, I'm with Venkman.
He got slimed!

That's great, Ray. Save some
for me.
FROM THE 1984 FILM
"GHOSTBUSTERS"

Oracles

> *The reasonable man adapts himself to the world:*
> *the unreasonable one persists in trying to adapt the*
> *world to himself. Therefore, all progress depends on the*
> *unreasonable man.*
>
> GEORGE BERNARD SHAW

One thing's for sure: As we approach the millennium, it seems definitely unreasonable to believe in oracles.

An oracle is a disembodied prophet (or a very wise deity) speaking through a human who may or may not go into a trance during the process. This is a method of divination in which specific inquiries are made and usually answered in sometimes fuller and deeper (but also sometimes more cryptic) fashion than one bargained for. The word "oracle" originally referred to the actual place where the gods passed on their wisdom, and eventually it became the term for the person who spoke the words and gave the messages. As is true of many forms of divination, the use of oracles to pass on wise words has been around forever. In ancient Rome and Greece oracles were consulted on an almost daily basis for important political and military advice. Sometimes the human forms through which they spoke were called sibyls, women priestesses who resided in caves.

Perhaps the most famous of the oracles were those at Delphi, where petitioners were chosen by lottery and then required to pay a fee for the privilege of an inquiry; they ranged from the leaders of the country to the common populace. The Delphic Oracle was understood to be the embodiment of the god Apollo, and her job was to provide guidance and authority in situations where mere reason and knowledge wouldn't do—wasn't enough. Tell that to King Croesus of Lydia, who led his brave soldiers to defeat when he asked the Oracle at Delphi for her thoughts. She told him a great army would be destroyed but never mentioned it would be *his* great army.

Oracles were omnipresent in Egypt starting around 2689 B.C. and in China as far back as recorded history takes us. Today Tibet is still a grand repository for oracles—and some are even designated as state oracles. Many think that modern Christian priests are respected as oracles because they enjoy a superior communication with God, who, through the priest, gives advice and answers to personal conundrums.

In cities across America, very few call themselves oracles; it's simply not au courant. Calling upon an oracle's services in Ho-HoKus, New Jersey, really requires one to suspend belief, let alone any hope of scientific methodology, as a means of unraveling nature's mysteries. Critics say that anyone who suspends belief deserves what she gets. Proponents of oracle sessions (as some have come to be known) say that the knowledge received and the psychic experience is meaningful whether or not a paranormal event has actually occurred. Even if the messages received originated from a wise human who is not disembodied at all and not an infallible disembodied entity, or even if the messages come from one's own unconscious mind, perhaps they still have great value if you feel they do.

The Oracle

PAMELA MILLER/MONGKA

So a good friend suggests I see an oracle. Will this require a trip to Delphi? No. Apparently an oracle lives among us on West Ninetieth Street in Manhattan. I want to keep an open mind, I want to remember that I've come to believe we are all, past and present, somehow connected . . . but an oracle? This one's hard. To be perfectly frank, of all the paranormal genres, this seems the nuttiest. To make things even more difficult, this oracle is also a channeler, although unlike most trancegoing channelers, she stays fully conscious as she communicates with her *entity*—a spirit guide from India—and he speaks through her. I will actually be able to hear Mongka's words (he's the true oracle) coming from Pamela Miller's (not her real name) mouth.

In my mind I keep thinking of Mongka as Mowgli, but no, I keep reminding myself—Mowgli's the little kid from the Kipling stories. Mongka, I've never met, even in the pages of a book. Well, I'm about to.

This is the real problem: I'm *so sure* it's a phony bit; how will I ever keep from giggling?

Well, Pamela Miller the oracle/channeler wants to meet me a week before the session, and I agree, even though I'm a little miffed. Look—I'm doing a book here, I'm a busy woman, no

time, no time, let me just get to the real thing. But no—she asks
me to come in to talk first.

A week before the oracle session, I visit Pamela.

She's tall and chic, with soft brown hair tucked behind her ears.
We sit and talk on white furniture, and in the background is a
gentle but persistent sound, a chant, really.

"It's a Sanskrit mantra—the Om Namah Shivayah," says
Pamela. "Om is the primordial sound, the first sound that the unmanifest makes as it manifests. Nama is a word of honor, and
Shivayah is the name of God. When we repeat the mantra, we're
reminding ourselves of our own divinity, the divinity of everything."

This is just what I was afraid of. Manifest, unmanifest, primordial . . . I can't stand it when people talk like that.

So I get down to business. And Pamela does also. She doesn't
say "unmanifest/manifest" again.

Am I going to laugh, I ask Pamela, when Mowgli—I mean
Mongka—makes an appearance? How are you going to be able to
prove to me that a spirit entity is speaking through you? Am I going to feel embarrassed in your group session?

She considers my questions seriously.

"You might," she says with great sweetness. She's not at all pa-
tronizing. "On the other hand, you might just be able to relax and
let me guide you in a meditation. You might be able to prove to
yourself that you are experiencing something beyond the obvious
levels of reality—because the burden of proof is on *you*, not me or
Mongka," she answers.

"The other day I saw a cartoon," she continues with a laugh.
"It was of two hand puppets, with one saying to the other, 'Sometimes I doubt that there's a hand.' Often people come here ex-

pecting some kind of phenomenal experience to *prove* the existence of an unseen spirit—room vibrations, the touch of a hand on their shoulders. Do we have to have something that's not quantifiable, quantified to make it real? People ask me all the time if I believe all this, if I can prove all this," continues Pamela. "A Buddhist would say, 'It's not a matter of belief. You do the practice and you have your experience and you have your proof.' "

Okay. But can you tell me who Mongka is and what to expect at the session next week? I ask.

"Mongka is a great being who is not in a physical body," Pamela answers directly. "I go into a deep meditation—not a trance—and I make an inner connection with him; it's an experience of merging. And then he speaks, and often he heals. Years ago in oracle group, one woman told Mongka, 'I don't know what I'm doing here, I don't even believe in God.' And he talked to her about how it's easier, if you don't have a belief in God, *if* you also don't have a disbelief, because then you're truly open to what's revealed to you."

At that point, continued Pamela, the lights in the room "altered, undeniably. Mongka paused when it happened to give her time to experience it and then said, 'See? What can God do to prove His existence?' The woman told us afterward that she felt extraordinarily peaceful from the exchange," says Pamela.

So what is Pamela's part? I ask.

"Simple. I help people recognize their *knowing*. I train people to notice what's happening on a very subtle level and to have confidence in their own powers of perception. How many times have you said, 'I *knew* I shouldn't have called her now,' or, 'I *know* there's a guardian angel near me.' Well, I help people to follow their *knowing*. That's spirituality. It's very practical, very pragmatic, not airy-fairy at all; it makes sense to include spirituality in our lives."

Is all this part of the paranormal world? I ask Pamela.

Again she considers. "I think of it as very normal," she answers. "I think it's abnormal to pretend there's no inner life. That sounds very odd to me, indeed. This voice, this body, this emotional affect, are not all we are; the level of reality on which you and I are conscious of relating right now is a very small part of reality. Where do we go when we sleep? The appreciation of deity is a spiritual and practical achievement—what's paranormal about that?"

Pamela says, "If something doesn't feel right, we have to trust ourselves to *know* that it probably isn't right. See how Mongka feels to you."

The morning of the oracle session arrives. I enter Pamela's living room to gentle chants playing in the background. Six other people, five women and a young man—they're regulars at the weekly oracle session, I discover—are already seated on the floor and in chairs. Candles are burning, but, thank goodness, we seem to be minus the incense, which always reminds me of the white-robed men who peddle the stuff on the street corners of New York. No one looks like a crazy—but, hey, you never know. The young man is probably a student, a very pregnant woman has the tousled golden hair of a Raphaelite painting—we seem to be of many ages. A kindly gray-haired woman asks me if I'd prefer the floor or a chair, and because my back is giving me grief, I choose a straight-back chair. The woman puts a pillow under my feet and behind my back, and to my surprise, the pain I've been living with for three weeks seems to dissipate. So far, I'm batting 1,000. I look around: everyone is sitting very straight, their hands either cupped, palm up in each other, or palm up resting at their sides. I sit very straight, too. I cup my hands, one in the other. I feel very spiritual. For about five minutes. Then I feel itchy.

No one talks for about fifteen minutes. Almost everyone's eyes

are closed. Hmm—this appears to be serious meditation, something at which I invariably fail. I can't sit *still* for long. I can't quiet
my mind for long. But, finally, finally, I let go—sort of let go, anyway. And the mind chatter slows down. Just do this right, Sherry,
I tell myself. Give it a chance.

Finally Pamela quietly enters the room and sits straight and
cross-legged on the white couch in front of us. Quietly she talks
us through to more relaxation, asking us also to sit tall, relax, relax, relax. . . .

And then—more quiet. I'm into it now. Eyes closed. I can do
this.

All of a sudden—"Welcome, welcome, welcome," says a voice
that's Pamela's but not Pamela's. Startled, I open my eyes and
see—Pamela. But there's no mistaking it: she's different somehow.
And from her mouth comes a sweet, higher voice with the tiniest
Indian accent. Mongka.

I close my eyes again and listen.

*Welcome to you. Experience the vibration of truth deep within
your own heart. In the very center of the cave of the heart, there is a
great openness. If you allow yourself to open into the stillness, you will
receive the pulsation of truth. Perceive the subtle vibration, the pulsation of truth. When you feel that you are losing ground, that you have
fallen away from your center, take a moment to reconnect with this
vibration. To one whose eye is open, this pulsation is everywhere, but
you must find your stillness.*

I *do* feel stilled.

Mongka speaks directly to the young man sitting on the floor
in front of me.

Do you have any questions, Robert?

Robert says, "I do, Mongka. During the day, when stress hits, how can I hold the stillness?"

You cannot hold it. Let it hold you. Just remember it. Healing begins so simply. The memory cherished easily becomes the experience itself. There is a stillness that pervades even restlessness. Put aside frustration—or slide through it. Do you have any questions, Sherry?

I do. I say that I feel Mongka—or Pamela—or someone has given me some kind of *authorization* to just stop, to let go my frenetic pace, to stop worrying about my family, this book, my new magazine article, getting everything *right*.

Then I feel quiet. I also feel this—pulsation. Pulsation? Nonsense. Talk about suggestive susceptibility. Then I fall into the pulsation—a kind of soundless, rhythmic vibration. It feels good, and I don't feel dumb.

And I say to Mongka, "I'm happy that you give me permission to stop, but I don't know how to give myself permission to stop."

I think I'm blathering. But it's okay. She/He understands.

Are you the authority that makes you keep going?

"Yes," I whisper.

Is it by your conscious choice that you live on overdrive?

"Yes."

If that were true, my dear, you would be able to shut it off, wouldn't you . . . if it were your conscious choice?

"Yes."

So, you only think you have control. Contemplate how little control you have. Confront that reality squarely, yet gently. Understand that in truth, your life is a partnership with something you don't consciously know. Do you understand?

"Yes."

I really do seem to understand what this person/Pamela/Mongka seems to be saying, and it's a great relief to hear that I don't have to control all the damn time: control my successes, control my destiny. All that controlling gets me so tired. I have never seemed to realize it before.

Develop your relationship, Sherry, with that which you have ignored for so long, and all will be revealed in time. It is very important to pay homage to time. Whatever it is you wish to attain, whether it is simply a goal to accomplish an amount of work or whether it is the attainment of a state, you must honor time. Make friends with time. It is so pragmatic to keep the company of this divine pulsation which is closer to you than your own breath.

Now, what *is* this? It all sounds like gobbledygook in the translation, but as it happened, as Pamela/Mongka spoke, the words resounded with clarity. Look, intellectually I am just not buying this, but emotionally it makes perfect sense to me. I do have to learn to respect or "make friends with" time. I am always running out of it. I am always racing against it. The idea of making friends with my enemy is peaceful. This Mongka is not too shabby a thinker. Or entity, whatever he is.

A woman asks, "How can I remember God when I get so far away from the experience?"

How do you remember your children when they're far away?

Is God so different? Perhaps the question is not how can you re-member, but how can you forget? Still, the mind is forgetful. But just as you needn't remember to breathe, so God permeates your life whether you recognize it or not. Take your safety from that under-standing. Is that clear?

"Yes," says the woman with a smile. She appears relieved.

"Are you a woman or a man?" asks someone else.

Mongka giggles—I swear it's a giggle.

"I don't know," he/she answers. "Is it important?"

It doesn't seem to be.

The very pregnant woman says that she feels great stress, and although she's trained herself to be patient, the impending birth has put distance between her and her husband. She feels so alone sometimes. And where is God, then? she wants to know.

Mongka seems to be getting a bit irritated.

It's important, Lara, that you know there is no distance between you and God. It's imperative that you develop this habit—now. All this training—for what? Just as your baby will reach reflexively for her mother's milk, reach inward for God's nurturance. Have that de-pendence on your own divinity! Devotion has this power to heal and sustain, and the distance from your husband will close.

The pregnant woman grins. A grin? That seems inappropriate. But speaking to her after the session, I understand.

"I don't see these sessions so much as mystical as practical," she tells me. "I feel it helps me to lead my life in a different way. Look—about what Mongka said. Becoming a mother is sort of forcing me to decide whether I want to choose God or the fear I feel when I have petty arguments with my husband. I can respond to the fear I have when Bill and I have a fight, or I can respond to God. Well, today, Mongka told me to choose my heart—not fear."

I tell Lara that it's the word "God" that throws me. What if a person's not religious?

"Say God, or substitute 'heart,' or 'soul,' or 'Something Else Out There' or whatever you want," answers Lara. "If you must know"—she smiles—"I never knew the meaning of the word 'God' until I started these sessions with Mongka. But the more I say it, the more I connect with something beyond me. And I see a positive change in me and my husband—although sometimes we seem to regress."

An older woman agrees. "I don't even think about Mongka as an entity—or even God as God. All I know is that I feel a great energy coming from the words coming from Pamela's mouth. And I, in turn, feel so energetic. I come for the energy. It's a great luxury to come here."

Do you think there's a *being* talking through Pamela? I ask Lara. She thinks. "It's just not important, not relevant anymore," she says. "But I think I do see Mongka and Pamela as separate, even though I derive great strength from Pamela herself, her sweetness, her wisdom. Whatever."

Whatever. Now, if I were reading this, I'd smirk. Whatever, indeed. This writer has been seduced, I'd think. Mind control, I'd think. Silly. Hypnotized.

But I'm writing it, not reading it. And I feel I want to go back someday. What happened? I don't know. Just that since that morning I seem to feel less *hustled* by what I previously would have looked at as opportunities lost. I'm not rushing around as much. I allow myself to read more than I have in past months and eat Hershey's bars—and I haven't done that for a lot of years. Even if a paranormal event has not actually occurred, the experience has been meaningful. And I'll remember it.

The people in the room with me were asking personal as well as quasi-religious questions that seemed to add up to Why are we here? and Where are we going? Mongka's answers were part sci-fi, yes, but also enormously thought jogging and gentling. It seems to me that anything that inspires one to find balance and comfort in life is worth pursuing, and if that balancing act is predicated on a belief that there are existences beyond the senses, consciousnesses beyond the body and the material world—than why not go for it, even though the tiny voice in my head is jeering: "*Sherry—an infallible, disembodied, ancient entity? C'mon!!*"

Is there a Mongka? I wouldn't swear to it—but I wouldn't swear there wasn't, either.

One month later I go back, this time with Carol and Stephanie, two good friends. I want to test my senses. Did I see what I thought I saw, hear what I thought I heard?

But Mongka's a no-show. Everything else is the same, Pamela's disciples (because that's how I've come to think of them) sit straight in a yogalike posture at her feet, the background chant is intoxicating. Carol and Stephanie and I are on straight-back chairs, the little pillows under our feet.

Pamela enters, sits cross-legged on the couch in front of us, and leads us in a meditation. She sounds like Pamela, but every now and then there's that slight lilt of an Indian accent entering her quiet voice. She tells us to feel the pulsing, feel the deep heart vibrations, feel the divine. Wants us to ask a question of our hearts. I keep waiting. No Mongka.

It's been almost an hour—I've peeked at my watch, and crazily,

I feel disappointed. Mongka was nice. Also, what *is* this—she's supposed to be an *oracle!* Am I being fooled? And although the meditation is pleasant, I keep waiting. Still, no-show Mongka. So I do a very bad thing—but *I have to.* I disturb the meditation and ask a question of Pamela. It's hard to do. I think everyone will feel annoyed at me.

"This room feels empty, Pamela," I say. "It was full when Mongka was here."

"Maybe you imagined it all," she whispers. "It's better if your heart is full than the room be full."

And that's all. We sit quietly in the dark for a little while, and then she asks me to turn on the light. I feel disappointed. . .

. . . and then surprised when everyone starts talking about their experiences in the last hour. No one mentions what, to me, is blatantly missing. One by one everyone describes a little about what's happening in her life and how clear she feels after this last hour. My own friends seem quiet, but they also speak to Pamela, describing their meditational experience.

Why is everyone ignoring this thing? Why won't anyone put words to it? Before we leave I approach Pamela. Please, tell me what happened, I say. Not mystically, but in *words.*

I don't know, she answers. One day I opened my mouth for Mongka and only Pamela spoke.

And that's *it.*

I talk to the regulars as we leave. Mongka hasn't been around for weeks, but not one person is unhappy about the no-show. Each still feels that she's gotten what she came for, a strength, a wisdom, a quietness.

In the taxi going home, Carol tells me a secret she didn't want to share with "all those strangers."

"I don't know if I felt any pulsing, any vibration," she begins, "but there was *something*. Maybe it was the candle flickering. And when Pamela said, 'Go below the surface, to the bottom of your awareness'—I tried to do it.

"I don't know if you know," Carol said quietly, "but I have a breathing problem. I can't get a deep breath. So, that's the question I asked of my heart: What the hell is this thing that's tying a knot in my lungs, stopping me from deep breaths? And then, I have to tell you, I was astounded. My mother materialized in my head as a young woman, in a forties sundress. I saw her clearly. She was saying, 'Let go of me, stop hanging on to me, you're always hanging on to me.' I wasn't ready, but in my mind I let go of the pretty woman in the sundress. And I took a deep breath, the first in a long time. Now? I feel great relief. You know what I think, Sherry? I think the oracle is within us. The presence you've been talking about, Mongka, who needs him? Mongka is bullshit. What's not bullshit is what happened in that room. We shouldn't look to mystics from India. We already have all the information about ourselves—and no one else has it. How can anyone but we save ourselves? What Pamela did is make me realize that the wisdom of the ancients is within us all. For me, this was a good evening."

Well, okay. But I still don't feel satisfied.

The next day Stephanie calls me.

"I think that Pamela is wholly earnest," she says. "I think she deeply understands that we're in the presence of the divine when we tap into ourselves, draw on a larger current within *ourselves*. Look—I believe that there's nothing obscure about all this. I know that there definitely are discarnate wise people—so what's the big deal if they're not around every time we want them? We want our priests to give us leadership, to take us where we have to go, but sometimes we're guilty of wanting theater, *performance,* a charismatic circus act.

"It's something like that Hebrew prohibition against idols. I think Pamela was steering all of us, but particularly you, from idolatry. I think she wanted us all to feel a sense of reverence and love without the *theater,* a sense of the divine in ourselves. You were too taken with the Indian entity. Oh, I know, it's very complicated."

It is. Who wouldn't be taken by a disembodied Indian entity? I ask you? But if Pamela was purposely perpetuating a fraud in saying she was an oracle through which an entity spoke, why didn't she just continue? She knew I was writing a book. Wasn't she taking an awful chance just changing the rules without explaining them to me?

Or are Carol and Stephanie right? Is she who she is and Mongka who He/She is and the divine oracle in all of us?

I like *definite.* This is a hard book to write.

Past-Life Regression

> *What if you slept? And what if, in your sleep, you dreamed? And what if, in your dream, you went to heaven and there plucked a beautiful flower? And what if, when you awoke, you had the flower in your hand? Ah, what then?*
> SAMUEL TAYLOR COLERIDGE

And what if *you* had the most powerful memory of another life, another time? What then? Would you have to insist you'd dreamed it?

Harper's Encyclopedia of Mystical and Paranormal Experience calls past-life regression "the remembering of alleged previous lives." A psychoanalyst I know calls it a "metaphorical reconstruction from the subconscious." My cousin who experienced it calls it weird.

There are events, real or imagined, that transform the way we think; they defy explanation. The sense of past-life regression is one of those events.

Have you ever traveled far from your home to a place you'd never before visited and felt as if you'd been there before?

Have you ever seen a house that, upon entering, you knew as well as you knew your own bedroom? You knew the actual *layout* of the house—where the kitchen, where the bathroom, was: you were *home?*

Have you ever known anyone who said he'd inexplicably begun to think or talk in a foreign language—one with which he'd had no previous familiarity?

Have you ever heard of a small child (in almost all documented cases, children who do this have been between ages two and five) who began talking about a past life and past friendships—perhaps in a different language?

Such people exist. Perhaps that's why, in the history of humankind, going back to the most ancient cultures, every one save our own modern Western culture has accepted reincarnation as an absolute. Even so, estimates have it that two-thirds of the world's modern population, including Egyptians, Africans, and North and South Americans, believe in reincarnation. Certainly ancient and modern Eastern religions—in particular Hindu and Buddhist—recognize past-life regression. In fact, says Leslie Austin, Ph.D., a past-life recall therapist, "Tibetan Buddhists are the astronauts of the inner world."

Assume we have had past lives: can we remember them? Although most traditions say that forgetfulness of past lives is necessary to the process of reincarnation, people who claim they can recall past lives are not unusual. As early as the second century B.C., Patanjali, the Indian yoga philosopher credited with compiling the *Yogasutras,* said that details of past lives exist in the subconscious mind and can be awakened through yoga and meditation. One of the first documented cases is that of Katsugoro (born in 1815), the illiterate, nine-year-old son of a poor Japanese farmer. He'd certainly never read a book, nor had he been taken out of his small village, so there was no way he could have learned the things of which he spoke. At the age of four he started telling his sister that he'd died in 1810 of smallpox at the age of six; he described the remote village he then lived in, his house, his parents, his death, and his burial. An investigation confirmed that everything he described was so.

Arguably America's most famous past-life recaller was Bridey Murphy. In 1952 a Colorado businessman and amateur hypnotist tried to help Virginia Tighe, a twenty-nine-year-old housewife, regress to past lives. To their mutual amazement, she had the strongest feeling she'd been Bridget (Bridey) Murphy, who lived in County Cork, Ireland, in the late 1700s to the mid-1800s. The uproar was enormous, critics declared a giant hoax, but even after investigations, no one could ever figure out how the woman who never frequented libraries knew so many tiny but vivid and accurate details of early-nineteenth-century Ireland.

In the twentieth century remembrances of lives past have come about primarily through hypnosis, but also through dreams, visions, or even physical traumas—like blows to the head.

Children especially are said to remember past lives, say some experts, because their past-life memories have less difficulty getting through the "awake" state.

In the West, belief in past-life recall has slowly increased to the point where it's being used by some psychotherapists. It generally works like this: Via hypnosis and gentle guided imagery, patients are encouraged to find their way through to another time or place in which they may have lived. Sometimes, making lists of aversions helps to provide pivotal clues to past lives. One woman who couldn't bear turtleneck sweaters or scarves of any type thought she'd discovered that she'd been hung in another life; finding that out, she says, erased her aversion to tight things around her neck.

Past-life regression therapy has become so popular, it has its own California-based organization—the Association for Past Life Research and Therapies (APRT), which was started in 1980. Although the group claims to have over nine hundred members consisting mostly of therapists interested in past-life therapy, the group is not heavy on quality control; it includes many dubious New Age practitioners and at least one doorman.

One of its members, though, has credentials impeccable enough to make the American Medical Association very happy. Brian Weiss, M.D., author of the best-selling *Many Lives, Many Masters* and *Through Time into Healing,* is a magna cum laude graduate of Columbia University and Yale Medical School, the ex-chairman of psychiatry at Miami's Mt. Sinai Medical Center, and a practicing psychoanalyst with a waiting list a mile long. Personal experiences in his own life and in those of his patients convinced this once skeptical physician to join the growing rank of analysts who practice past-life regression as therapy.

It started for Weiss in 1980 when a young woman named "Catherine" began treatment with him. She suffered from intense fears, phobias, and panic attacks that did not respond to eighteen months of traditional therapy. Frustrated, Weiss decided to hypnotize her. As she regressed to the age of five, she recalled that she almost drowned in a swimming pool. Regressed to age three, she remembered her father's drunken, sexual molestation. Regressed to age two, she remembered nothing. Then, on a hunch, Weiss asked her to "go back to the time when your symptoms arise." Instantly Catherine was flooded with memories from many different past lives.

She recalled drowning in a flood in 1863 B.C., having her throat cut as a young boy in the Netherlands in 1473, and dying from a water-borne epidemic in eighteenth-century Spain. With each subsequent memory and session, another of Catherine's anxieties died.

For Weiss personally, this was to be much more than a patient's breakthrough. In one session Catherine began speaking to the doctor in a husky voice. "Your father is here and your son, who is a small child," the husky-voiced Catherine told Dr. Weiss. "Your father says you will know him because his name is Avrom and your daughter is named after him. Also, his death was due to his heart. Your son's heart was also important, for it was backward, like a chicken's. He made a great sacrifice for you, out of love. He wanted to show you that medicine could only go so far, that its scope is very limited."

The information stunned Weiss. His father, Alvin, was a religious Jew who was far better suited to his Hebrew name of

Avrom, and he had died of heart disease—and yes, Weiss's daughter was named for him. But the crusher was this: Catherine had spoken of the greatest tragedy of Weiss's life—the death of his firstborn son, Adam, eleven years earlier, who indeed had a heart that was turned around, like a chicken. When open-heart surgery failed to save the baby, Weiss decided against a career in internal medicine. Convinced that modern medicine could go only so far, he opted instead for psychiatry. Weiss was a specialist in brain chemistry, but the information that Catherine offered went far beyond chemistry, far beyond the five senses. "A hand had reached down and irreversibly altered the course of my life," says Weiss. "My mind was now open to the possibility, even the probability, that Catherine's utterances were real."

Although past-life recall has been around for centuries, the use of it in therapy is brand new, says Weiss. "You don't have to be dysfunctional or even have symptoms to benefit from past-life therapy," says Dr. Weiss. "You don't even have to believe in it—not the therapist *or* the patient. It works whether you believe or disbelieve."

But is it real—or is it the conjuring up of powerful metaphors to shed light on problems in the same way our dreams shed light on buried thoughts during traditional psychoanalysis?

"I think it's very real," says Dr. Weiss. "A real memory. Sometimes it may start out as a patient's construct—a symbol or a metaphor or even an instance of vivid imagination; most often, all those things are first mixed together, as in a dream. But the more the patient does, the more often *real* memories of past lives return. And when it comes to therapy, it doesn't even matter whether it's real or not, because people get better. I think it's related to the new field of psychoneuroimmunology, in which patients can marshal the immune system to fight diseases with the mind.

"The huge irony is that past-life therapy is so very close to traditional Freudian therapy."

But is it scientific?

"The core premise of science is to observe without bias or prejudice—then you can see clearly," says Weiss. "You test a premise, others test it, it works, the premise becomes a theory. The most unscientific attitude is to have an opinion about something you know nothing about, something you haven't tried. To say that past-life regression is quackery without studying it is the opposite of science."

Critics abound.

Some say that past-life regressions are directly influenced by the will and bias of the therapist and the patient's own interests and concerns, which is why a person with an interest in Greek literature will find herself living in Plato's republic.

Some say that the subconscious of the patient makes up stories to relieve him of blame and guilt; it's easier to say that he was a wife beater in 1700 than confess to the overpowering desire to hit his wife in 1996.

But even if you think of past-life therapy as a kind of dreamwork, a metaphor, it can be extremely useful, say practitioners. It teaches one to dig into the resources of one's mind, memory, and imagination for clues about deepest feelings.

The Past-Life Regressor

Failing to fetch me at first keep encouraged,
Missing me one place search another
I stop somewhere, waiting for you
WALT WHITMAN

LESLIE AUSTIN, PH.D.

I KNOW THIS ISN'T GOING TO WORK. And I tell it to Leslie Austin, Ph.D., past-life regression counselor.

Apparently, although I don't realize it, I've already said it about five times during our presession interview.

"Don't feel bad if nothing happens—no one has ever been able to put me under hypnosis, and I doubt I'll really experience a past life," I announce. "Anyway, I have my mind on writing it all up for my book," I say. "So, I'm working during the experience; that will probably break my concentration."

As we're about to start, I give her another version of that speech. Then she smiles and finally responds, "So, okay, that's fine, Sherry, we'll start with just that: How come you're working when you're supposed to be experiencing?"

I know she's got me. Often I hide behind a journalist's mask instead of jumping into life, into *feeling*. I guess it's a safety belt— "hey, look, this isn't really me *doing* all these crackpot things; I'm just observing them for the story!"

But you want to know the truth? Not one inch of my rational mind believes I'm going to remember having lived some other time in some other place.

That's okay with the past-life counselor.

"Sometimes people come to me as professed believers in this work with the most narrow-minded perspective of what they expect, and *they're* the biggest pain in the butt to work with," she says with a grin. "Being a believer is not even an issue. The question is, are you willing to have an experience of self-examination that may or may not reveal things you want to know about yourself in order to grow happier? The experience is all," says Leslie.

But I know it's a problem. I find that I approach each new paranormal genre with enormous resistance. It's very, very hard to be open, and I know that my attitude may be a real block to having the experience—even if such things exist. Some experts feel that the emotional link is critical to success. Dr. Gertrude Schmeidler, a professor at City College in New York, began investigating ESP while a research associate at Harvard University, and her first experiment is now a classic. She separated people by their attitudes toward ESP: the "sheep" who believed in ESP and the "goats" who disbelieved. She found that believers scored consistently higher than the disbelievers, who consistently scored below chance. In other words, to receive the experience, the person must be receptive, say many experts. Even Jung acknowledged this by writing, "The test person either doubts the possibility of knowing something one cannot know or hopes it will be possible and that the miracle will happen. At all events, the test person being confronted with a seemingly impossible task finds himself in the archetypal situation, which so often occurs in myths and fairy tales, where divine intervention, i.e., a miracle, offers the only solution."

There are three ways to look at past-life therapy, Leslie tells me. "You can say, as I deeply believe, that it's literal and real and there's a soul that continues that preexists the present body and lives on after the body dies. Most really good practitioners work from that frame of reference.

"Other therapists are willing to say that past-life therapy is only a spiritual metaphor. If you accept that frame of reference, past-life work is like doing dreamwork: it's a story you come up with from your own psyche about yourself. But even if you want to say your past-life recall is not about real life, but only about imagination, there's still a particularity about it—why *that* lifetime, why *those* events—what does your metaphoric story say about the way you live in the world? This is very helpful in getting yourself unstuck from places in which you're stuck, in seeing the patterns of how you live and the beliefs that shape your actions."

And, says Dr. Austin finally, there are many people who travel in past-life recall as "tourists who are simply following an intellectual challenge—and that's fine, also. Think how fascinating it is!

"However you approach past-life regression, it should culminate in a flowering of the soul. Even if you don't need it to heal yourself in the sense of repair, you can use it for the fruition of the future."

I think I'm willing. But even if I regress to another life, how will I explain that kind of embarrassing miracle to my even more skeptical children, friends, husband? How will I explain it to myself? Is it possible for me to suspend skepticism after a lifetime of skepticism?

Okay, okay. I'll try. I'll try for the miracle. I settle down into a deep leather lounge in a room that's filled with golden Buddhas, totem poles from New Guinea, leering masks, and Mario Buatta–y chintz wing chairs.

Leslie tells me not to worry about my inability to be hypnotized.

"There's nothing woo-woo here, nothing mysterious," she says. "While sometimes, deep hypnotic states are the only way to work with people who are disconnected from their selves, ninety-five percent of the time it's completely unnecessary. The model of hypnosis I use is the classic definition of hypnosis: it's simply an altered state of consciousness, a highly focused state, and getting into it is not a complicated phenomenon. When you're driving on a highway and you can't remember the last three minutes or when you go off into a daydream, a reverie—you're in a hypnotic state. I will tell you everything I'm doing as we go along. This is *your* experience, not mine, and there are no secrets. I'm here to guide you, not to program or shape your experience in any way."

She's as good as her word. Never at any time during the session I'm about to describe do I feel that Leslie has put words or thoughts into my mind. As she describes it, "I'll shine a flashlight into dark corners, but *you*'ll do the looking."

Why am I doing this, anyway? Why does anyone do it? I ask Leslie.

She says that we all have different affinities to different places in the world, different cultures that are not explainable by anything this life. It's one person's certain feeling of *home* in Paris. It's another's sense of *rightness* when he's in sight of mountains. Leslie tells me that insight into past lives may explain these emotional and spiritual sensations. It also may account for problems that trouble us in this life—it's a tool of understanding, besides being an extraordinary journey. She says that insight into past lives helps explain mysteries. One client, for example, was curious to know why, although she never took music lessons in her life, from the age of four she could listen to an orchestra playing and hear each instrument individually. Her regression took her to a life in which she'd been a conductor. "Why is it," asked one client, "that I went to England last summer and went nuts on the London Bridge—had a really terrible and frightening reaction of fear?" She discovered she'd lived near the Thames in the eighteenth century and was raped on the bridge. Another client confesses an almost obsessive fascination with clay—and she's not an artist. "But," says Leslie, smiling, "once she was."

Another reason for me to experience past-life regression: "If you're really hoping to widen your frame of reference through this book you're writing," says the therapist, "you'll want to go outside the five senses to a *truly* scientific model that includes all the intangible, invisible parts of yourself. Try to learn to trust your body," she says, "the experiences your body tells you are real—even if they're invisible for the moment. When you experience past life, your body will tell you what's real. Learn to trust it."

Then she gives me a short experiment to try, just before we begin the real journey.

"Check out your body—not your intellect," she instructs. "Imagine what you're going to have for lunch, next Friday. Make it vivid."

I conjure up a grilled-cheese sandwich in my mind.

"Now," instructs Leslie, "remember the last food you ate today. Recall it, make it vivid."

I taste the split-pea soup.

Leslie asks, "Which is more real? Is there a different *physical* experience when you think of the soup and when you think of the sandwich?"

Yes. I definitely salivated when I thought of the soup. I felt full. Thinking of the sandwich was only a perfunctory experience compared to the actual experience of the soup.

"You may think you're imagining things as you recall past lives," says Leslie, "but your body doesn't imagine, it doesn't lie. It will tell you the difference between what actually happened and what you're making up."

The therapist talks to me. She says she'll tell me what she's doing while she's doing it—no secrets, remember—and points out that, at the moment, she's trying to slow us down—change my worked-up interviewing mode to a more languid, contemplative pacing.

I like this. I like feeling privy to her methods, her intelligence; it makes me a partner into this exploration of unknown territories.

She begins to recap what we've already discussed, reminding me that I've said I always feel I have to put others at their ease, reassure them that it's okay if they fail—just as I did when I told her not to worry if I don't have past-life recall—it was *my* failure, not hers. We talk like that for a while. Then she says we need to be clear: if something *does* happen, should we progress deeply?

Oh yes, I say bravely.

So a past life *may* come up, she says, and we should progress if it does, but you're not at all sure it would come up, right? Right, I nod. Okay, she says. Then, very frankly, she asks:

"So, how come it wouldn't?"

Her directness is activating. It launches me into a discussion of my lifetime of skepticism and my mother, who taught me not to trust anyone who wasn't blood related.

"Trust me"—Leslie smiles—"even though I'm not your cousin. But notice how your energy level has risen?" she asks. "I'm going to talk with you until I feel truly live energy from you, until I get a really striking thought and feeling. Then I'm going to help you intensify the thoughts or the feelings. Then I'm going to ask you to notice body sensations. When I get all three of those things in sync—the thought, the feeling, the body sensations—that's the bridge into the past life: that's the *how.*"

I have to say it. Most critics simply say that past-life therapy has nothing to do with scientific methodology. I *like* science. What does Dr. Austin think about that?

Ask any scientist, says Dr. Austin, "to show you, in the realm of the five senses, where your emotions physically live in your body. Ask him to show you where your mind lives, where love lives, in the body. When scientists talk about methodology, they're usually talking about a system that works extremely well—in the realm of the five senses. Period.

"But," says Austin, "the soul lives. *The soul lives.*"

Then Austin tactfully suggests I zip my lips, close my eyes, and go inward for a while.

"Reflect on how being a skeptic and not believing anything you can't experience through your five senses has been good for you," she says.

I think. Perhaps skepticism is a way of aligning with my mother, staying connected with her, even though I criticized her constantly for the skepticism. I can even hear myself hissing to her—"Don't you ever trust *anyone?*"

"Already there's a theme that's emerging about separation and individuation," says Leslie. "I'm curious if that's a theme that runs through your life."

I sit up straight. It didn't take her long. Problems of separation seem to be an issue that's generational in my family. I immediately begin to discuss it with Leslie.

I remember sending my small daughter off on a camp bus and suffering—excessively, I now know—because no one sat next to her. The bus pulled out, I was left, and I cried; I remember the physical pain in my chest, and I remember thinking that the word "heartache" was more accurate than I dreamed. I couldn't bear being separated from my child in a place where I couldn't help, couldn't find another little girl to sit near her. I remember, fifteen years earlier, sitting on the steps of my sorority house in college and weeping because I'd witnessed some terrible cruelty to another young woman—and because I was a member of the group, I felt partly responsible for the meanness. But why I was *really* weeping, if you want to know the truth, was because my mom wasn't home for my telephone call so I could tell her about it. I felt so frustrated, so decimated, by the distance between us. Leslie was right. I don't do well with separation.

"You had a little 'a-ha!' there, didn't you," she says, and laughs. Then she tells me she notices that when I have a strong emotional connection to something, I appear to quickly take myself out of my *feeling* and put myself back into my *intellect*. She says it's okay, that I know more about myself than anyone else, and I use this as a survival technique—not, as most traditional therapists would label it, as a defense. Against what? We have to find out.

She asks me this question: "If you could know anything about yourself from a past-life context, what would you be curious to know?"

Like a shot, I have the answer. In a past life, if there is such a thing, did I ever do anything differently with my mother, with my grown children? Did I ever do it really *well?* So what worked then? I'm dying to know.

"Well, think. What *other* relationship could you have had with any of these people that's influencing your relationship now?"

We talk, we plod through, we search for sources of discordance, for carryovers from a past life. It's fascinating, this speculation, even though I'm far from convinced. I do feel a powerful kind of energy here. I would just *love* to know this: *Did* I know these people in my life before? Leslie tells me to go with the energy, to see if I feel it in my body. I do—I notice kind of a *whoosh*ing sensation, a little *airiness* in my chest. Then I analyze what I'm feeling. I may feel this airiness because I want this session to be more than it is, I say. I'm not giving you or anyone *enough* here. I feel guilty because I want to be terrific at this.

And Leslie helps me. "You want there to be more, you're not getting what you need, here in this room with me or in your relationships with your mom or your children? Right? Is that what's happening? You aren't giving me or them enough, is that what you said? You want this session to go somewhere, right?"

Yes, I admit. Number one, I want desperately to experience a past life if there is such a thing. Number two, it'll be better if I do so because then I'll have good copy for the book. But number three, am I crazy even to think that such things could be? Still, I don't *want* to hold back, I tell Leslie.

She's very reassuring. "Look—you're not alone in this feeling. Almost everyone does the same thing," she says. "My last client was experiencing a stabbing in a previous life, and even as she felt the pain of the knife, some part of her was saying, 'Give me a break—what is this, I'm making it all up!' It's the mind in a desperate struggle to control the world as we understand it to be. Don't worry about it, Sherry."

Then she tells me to ask the question. So I do. I don't know whom I'm asking it of, but I say it out loud.

Did I know my mom, my daughter, my son, in a past life? What was the source of our difficulties?

Say it louder, she tells me: Say, *"I really want to know."*

I ask it. I say it. Out loud. More than once. "I really want to know."

"Let yourself go back in time and space to another time to find the source. Something will pop up in your head. What pops up as you go back to the original moment of the difficulty between you and your mom? Something is happening around you. Describe it, even if you think you're making it up," says Leslie. "Describe it. Tell me. What's in your mind right now? Don't worry—it's okay to make it up."

As soon as she says it's okay to be "making it up"—I'm free. I see. Clear as day, I see—my body *feels*—a tug-of-war between someone who appears to be me—except I'm younger and I have light brown hair instead of black hair and—who is on the other end of the rope? Damn, I *can't see.*

Leslie helps. "Is it male or female?" she asks.

It's male. No question. A bigger boy.

"What's he wearing?" asks Leslie.

Maybe knickers, I say. But that's because I'm *sure* my imagination is working overtime and I want to put him in another time, another life. I am making up a story.

"What are you wearing on your feet?" asks Leslie.

Patent-leather Mary Janes. I see them, I really do. I'm not inventing this part. White socks. They tickle and they're falling down a little. Then I feel stupid.

"Is it *really* okay if I'm making this up?" I ask again.

"Yes," she says. "Very often in the very beginning," she explains, "we have to say we're making it up in order to give ourselves permission to go into another whole way of experiencing something. What will tell you if it's real or not is *after* the entire experience is over. You'll evaluate it later. Process it later. Now, go with the energy. Don't resist your self if your self wants to call it making it up. Honor yourself."

That seems to make sense. Leslie guides me through my vision. How much older is the boy? (Can't tell.) What kind of rope are we tugging? (I see it clearly—it's solid, not bendable, and it's looped around so it looks like a giant paper clip. It's rough—hurts my hand.) Am I winning in the tug? (No.) Do I give in when the boy pushes? (Never. I hold my ground or else I'll fall and *I don't want to fall.*) Where is this happening? (Seems like a meadow, maybe a playground without the playground equipment. It's green and flat, the terrain, it's hot out, the boy is stronger than I, I feel frightened and overpowered. It's a boy on the other end of the rope, but I feel my mother's presence. I do. Is the boy my mother in disguise?) I stop the picture.

Eyes closed, I confess to Leslie that I think I want her to know that I'm too sharp to fall for this sucker stuff—even though it does seem marvelously alive.

"Let's just acknowledge," she says quietly, "that it seems very important to you that you name and box and analyze every step of the way. It's okay. And what you're indeed feeling is a tug-of-war—just as you and I here are having a tug-of-war, very literally. And that's okay, too. You're absolutely convinced I'm going to pull you into an inauthentic experience. And you won't let it happen. Your metaphor is literal. You live in a tug-of-war, past life or this life. You get your way or someone else wins."

Yes, that's certainly true. She's good.

I keep my eyes closed. Leslie is silent. I'm relaxed.

So I go with it, let the scene change abruptly. I describe the new pictures, out loud; I know Leslie is listening, although now she's quiet. I'm alone, late afternoon, walking down a long, wooded path. I'm wearing sandals and something white and long. This place looks like camp. Green shade trees and orange salamanders on the banks of a narrow creek. In the background are vespers bells. *Vespers* bells? I don't even know what vespers *is*. No camp I ever went to had vespers. I bend down and reach into the creek and scoop up a salamander, expecting it to feel cool and slimy, but *shock*—it's hot and dry. Immediately my fingers are dry, dry, dry as dust. It's achingly familiar, but it just can't be real. Where am I? When is this? I stop the reverie.

I'm *really* making it up, I announce. Then I feel the irresistible impulse to lick the tips of my dry fingers, a persistent (to this day) childhood habit: after a hot bath or after my hands have been immersed even in cold water for any length of time, my fingers have always dried and puckered—and I need to lick them. They feel—they feel kind of like salamanders. Did this finger-drying business start a long time ago, with salamanders?

"It's okay," Leslie soothes. "It really is."

When I open my eyes I'm surprised to see Leslie—even though I knew she was there, all the time. I'm surprised not to see the meadow or the camp path. Vespers was nice, whatever it was. I feel as if I've come from a long way. At the same time, I also feel as if I've been role-playing—and I wasn't really anywhere. My sense is that Leslie led me to the top of a cliff—but never pushed me over. I am safe.

I look at my watch.

We've been at this almost two hours; I can't believe it. I know Leslie has another client due momentarily, and we have to stop. Reluctantly I let the little light brown–haired girl and the older boy go. I know she's me. Who is he? They seem as real as my right arm. I feel a sense of loss at letting them go. I let the dry orange salamander go.

But did I go back—anywhere? Were the wooded path and the salamanders from another life? What's with the long white dress and the golden sandals (yes, now I remember, they were golden)? Was the little boy with knickers from another time, and if he wasn't, why the knickers? I mean, I never saw a kid with knickers before, in this life. And where did my mother fit in? I feel as if the boy and I have been traveling through some time bends before—and we're not finished with the trip (trips?) yet. I think that I'd like to finish with him some other time. Even if it's role-playing and not real.

Later my agent, Connie, says the reason I didn't do *so* well in past-life regression is because my mother's voice stopped me short. My mother's voice told me that to think the same consciousness could exist in lifetime after lifetime is *naive,* and to think that even if it could, I could recapture it, is *wishful thinking.* I don't like to be disrespectful, says my agent, but could you please tell your mother to shut up?

Dowsing

Dark Underground
The Water Flows
In Hidden Veins That
No One Knows
Until the Forked Stick
Bends and Shows.
LOGO OF THE AMERICAN
SOCIETY OF DOWSERS
BOOKSTORE

Dowsing is an ancient art. Dating back some seven thousand years, it was originally thought to be only a tool of divination for the purposes of locating substances, people, animals, or objects. And a whole lot of people throughout history believed it worked.

Prehistoric wall drawings discovered in the Atlas mountains of North Africa depicted a person holding a forked rod made of hazel, ash, or willow wood, obviously searching for water. The theory is this: As the dowser comes close to the place where the water (or the gold, oil, or missing object) lies, the rod will twitch or bend or in some other way point to the exact direction the dowser ought to look. Dowsing rods, incidentally, have been called witch's sticks, wizard's rods, and worse by people like Martin Luther, who said dowsing was the work of the devil; to counteract these evil influences, early dowsers often baptized their sticks with Christian names. Calling a dowsing stick Father Jean made it lovable.

Ancient Egyptian art shows dowsers with their ubiquitous "Y" rods and their headdresses to which antennae have been added. There were dowsers in Caesar's army as it conquered Europe. Ancient Chinese kings used dowsing rods, and during the Middle

Ages dowsing was used to locate coal deposits in Europe and Great Britain.

Today, "new dowsing," as it is often called, is employed not only to find things, but also to diagnose disease, promote healing, locate noxious energies in homes, cars, and people, pick horses, speculate in stocks, discover archaeological ruins, forecast weather, and choose propitious times and places to hunt, fish, or farm.

The new dowsing rarely involves wooden sticks anymore; they've given way to copper and aluminum wires, iron, bronze, plastic, or steel rods and even bent coat hangers. Probably the most popular dowsing instrument is now the pendulum, usually a crystal or gemstone suspended on a chain that rotates and "points" in response to questions. Some people whip out their tiny dowsing pendulums in bookstores to see what books will have the most interest for them. Others won't buy a car or see a film without checking them out with a dowsing tool. Some oil, gas, and mineral companies use dowsers and claim a higher degree of accuracy than geologists using "scientific" techniques.

And the new dowsing is amazingly creative—*if* you buy it at all. New dowsers often work from a map or a printed "dowsers' chart," dowsing situations thousands of miles or even several lifetimes away. Soldiers in the Vietnam War were said to have used dowsing rods to locate booby traps and sunken mortar shells.

Although there are a million theories, nobody really knows *how* it works.

Most people think that psychic ability plays a key role and believe that a sixth sense in the dowser, some form of intuition, kicks in to concentrate on the water, lost object, missing person, or information the dowser seeks. Retrieved (but still on a subconscious level) information may then be translated to the dowsing tool by the dowser's subtle muscle vibrations: rods bend or twitch, pendulums swing, or, in "deviceless dowsing," arms and hands point—

and these divining tools pass on the information to a conscious level of the dowser. In a recent article in the prestigious *Smithsonian* magazine, writer Jack Hope notes that many of today's dowsers describe their talent as a "universal force" or as a "Jungian kind of superconsciousness." Other students of dowsing believe that dowsing rods are sensitive to electrostatic and electromagnetic fields that all substances give off. Still others believe that electrical fields can, through practice, become especially concentrated in the body. Since they contain both positive and negative charges, our bodies function as supersensitive receiving sets, and the concentrated energy causes the pendulum to move, the stick to bend.

Who can be a dowser? You, even I. Experiments have shown that almost anyone can learn to dowse and young children are particularly good at it. Experiments in Russia have demonstrated that dowsers can transmit their sensitivity to others merely by touching them while they dowse.

Literally, what happens when one dowses?

A dowser searching for water actually talks to his dowsing rod; he may say, "Please show me where I might find a vein of potable water that is not too far beneath the ground surface." The tip of his rod may then dip down toward the south or rise up expectantly toward the north. After the dowser follows in that general direction, the tip of the dowsing rod may suddenly point straight down, toward the earth. He's found his spot.

"Now, please tell me," the dowser may then ask in a series of yes/no questions, "is the potable water more than three hundred feet below the ground?" If the rod doesn't move, the dowser may ask, "Is the water fewer than three hundred feet belowground?" narrowing his options, question by question. (By long experience the dowser may have determined that a gentle sideways motion indicates a "yes" and a violent wiggle a "no"; each dowser depends on different signs from his instrument.)

In similar fashion, a New Age dowser using a pendulum poised over a pendulum chart (available in New Age bookstores) may ask a question of her pendulum. For example:

Which body part or ailment most needs attention? The pendulum may then swing to *circulation, blood pressure,* or *hiatus hernia* on the chart, among a multitude of possibilities.

Which exercise would most benefit me? The pendulum could swing to *jogging, walking,* or *swimming,* among a multitude of possibilities.

On a chart labeled "Allergy Problems," a dowser might ask, *What is most adversely affecting me now?* and choose from *soybean, eggs, cats, mold,* or *chocolate.*

I know, I know. But maybe we shouldn't knock it till we try it. Which we did.

The Dowser

ANNE WILLIAMS

LARRY AND I ARRIVE LATE to the dowsing workshop given by longtime dowsing counselor Anne Williams, a co-chairperson of the New York City chapter of the American Society of Dowsers— but no one pays any attention to our entrance: already a group of about sixty people is listening raptly. It looks like a pretty rational, eclectic group—varying in age and ethnic denominations—until I see the swinging *things*. What have I gotten into this time?

Picture it: Each person is holding a small pendulum suspended by a cord or a chain that looks to be between six and eight inches long; some of the pendulums look like pointed crystal chandelier drops, others like metal Life Savers or gemstones. As the workshop participants listen to Anne, they are, it seems, also fixated on these pendulums, swinging them in small arcs—and *muttering*. Okay—I've seen a lot of remarkable things lately, things beyond coincidence, but *this* makes me laugh. I am here, but I am not *of* these workshop participants.

I've always thought dowsing is the process of discovering hidden underground sources like water and oil with the use of a divining rod—a small, forked, stick. What's with the pendulums?

Anne, standing in front of a desk unaccountably cluttered with carrots and fruits, explains. She seems to be in her early sixties, with twinkly blue eyes and dark hair pulled back in a chignon that reveals tiny, red stone earrings. First, though, she asks the group to give itself "permission to see life in a different way." She tells us that when the rational mind gets in the way of the spiritual mind, it blocks access to marvelous powers. She instructs us to lay aside the rational mind—if only for a few moments.

Already this is getting me cranky. If I put aside my rational mind—what's left? Irrationality? Shouldn't a paranormal genre be able to coexist with a rational mind?

I pull myself up short and decide not to be a wise guy. If I've learned anything at all in this past year, it's to be patient—to wait and see, to keep an open mind. Down, hackles.

"We *are* going to keep open minds," I whisper to Larry.

"Trouble with open minds," he whispers back, "is that people fill them with junk."

I look around the room. There's a smart-looking Asian woman in a blue sweater, a guy wearing a shirt that says "POLO," a pretty gray-haired matron type, a Hispanic man who hangs on Anne's every word, a college kid in a "YALE" T-shirt. Are *all* these nice people loony? Maybe Anne means that there are powers or energy accessible by a sixth sense—a kind of intuition, spirituality, or ESP. If I rely only on logic and the usual five senses, I'm not giving this a fair chance. I seem to be saying that a lot lately.

Dowsing, says Anne, is traditionally used to detect water or underground objects, but today we know it can also be used to gain information and improve the quality of life in general. Traditionally, Y-shaped divining rods that would bend to indicate the presence of water *were* the instrument of choice, but today, says Anne, many people prefer pendulums, which are almost human in their capacity to point to solutions as well as to indicate yes or no responses. Dowsing, says Anne, "can extend your senses and reach anything in the universe, without limitations.

"It's beautiful! I've used it to get rid of headaches, find lost stuff, choose the vitamins I most need, and pick out great melons. Watch!" she says.

She picks up a small green apple that has been marked with an *O,* indicating an organically grown apple, and she holds her pointy wooden chestnut of a pendulum over the apple. "Is this a good apple for me to eat, one that is pure and has not been sprayed with pesticides?" she asks the pendulum. I feel slightly embarrassed for her.

The pendulum moves in a clockwise circle.

"That's a yes!" she exclaims. "Now, look carefully." She holds the pendulum over a brown, dented apple: it does not have an *O.* She asks the same question.

The pendulum begins to move counterclockwise.

Hmmm. I'm not impressed—although it's a good show. She's very good at this, and though I can't really swear to it, I know it's possible that she's moving the pendulum herself. Then, eyes twinkling, she knocks that theory out the window.

"*Sure,* I'm moving the pendulum—if that's what you're thinking—and that's fine. It's easier to get it started that way from a position of inertia. But I'm not moving it all the time. Don't let me try to convince you. Do it yourself—start a slight oscillation with your own pendulums and then let the natural force take over the pendulum's motion."

She passes around various onions and fruits and calls a five-minute break so those of us who don't have pendulums can choose one from an assortment on a table in the front of the room. I am drawn to a round, Austrian cut crystal suspended from a yellow cord: it feels cool and comforting in the hand, and I take it back to my seat. Larry chooses a turquoise gemstone on a metal chain.

We test our fruits. Some people seem satisfied that their pendulums are correctly diagnosing their bananas and oranges. Nothing much happens with Larry and me. We experiment with each other's pendulums. They just kind of *hover* over the fruit. We're moved to giggles.

Anne tells us that we will need to train our pendulums to work for us. It is best, she cautions, not to let anyone else use them so they can get used to our own particular energies, vibrations, and electrical fields. She gives us each a card with "Yes" printed on the right side and "No" printed on the left. As she instructs, we hold the pendulum over the card and clearly ask the pendulum to move clockwise toward the Yes for an affirmative/yes sign. It's okay, she repeats, to get the pendulum moving by slightly swinging it up and down vertically, at first.

"Tell the pendulum in no uncertain terms exactly what you want it to do. Think of it as a little person," she says. "Actually say, out loud, 'Move clockwise, little pendulum, to get to the Yes.' "

I have to say that as reluctant as I am to talk to pendulums, Larry is worse. He snickers and stares dourly at his turquoise. I try my crystal, holding the string between my thumb and index finger. "Move to the right, pendulum," I say self-consciously. At first it only continues in the up and down position in which I've started it out. Then—can it be, can it be?—the crystal, poised over the white card, moves slowly in a circular motion to the Yes area. I yelp in delight. Larry shakes his head disgustedly. Inspired and ignoring him, I say, "Move to the left, little guy."

The pendulum turns counterclockwise.

Stupefied, I stare at it.

"If you're not doing it on purpose," Larry says, "your intent is subconsciously making it happen."

It seems as if Anne is eavesdropping—but she can't be from thirty feet away. "If you're worried that you're subconsciously making it happen," she comments, "close your eyes when you work. It's harder to fool yourself."

Her voice comes over the mutterings of the other workshop participants (and now I'm muttering, too, as I exhort the round, glittery crystal pendulum).

"Ask the pendulum some clear questions answerable in 'yes' or 'no' to test it," she says.

"Is it raining in this room?" I ask my crystal. The pendulum swings counterclockwise, *by itself, I swear it.*

"Should I take calcium supplements?" I ask. The pendulum swings clockwise to Yes. My doctor has recently advised likewise.

"You try it, smart aleck," I tell Larry.

Now, before I tell you about Larry's question, I should mention that we have a fishing boat and Larry loves it beyond all things, except *maybe* me. He wants to spend a whole lot of money putting radar ($2,000), an electric toilet ($900), and two new engines ($25,000) on this boat. I am not thrilled with this idea, especially the $25,000 part.

"Should I buy a new toilet and radar for the boat?" asks Larry. The pendulum swings to Yes. He grins.

"Should I buy new engines?" he asks. The pendulum swings to No. I grin.

Anne's voice pulls the group back to her.

"The pendulum can be used not only to find things or answer your questions, but as an energy force," she says. "You can make things happen with a pendulum if you work at it. But it is best," she warns, "to clear all negative energy fields from your pendulum. Before each session that you use it, say the following—or something like it:

Please do not allow my thoughts, wants, or personal needs to get in the way of accuracy with my dowsing. Do not allow any negative forces to work through me at any time. Please send me a perfect polarity balance. Surround me with a great abundance of white light and loving healing energy. Allow the questions I ask to be for my highest good and my intentions to be clear."

The workshop lasts for hours. We take turns dowsing ourselves and each other. The YALE kid dowses up the keys he's been looking for all week: after a series of questions he's asked his pendulum—"Are they somewhere in the street?" No. "At home, then?" Yes! "In my bedroom? in a dresser? under the bed? in a closet? in my jeans? in my leather jacket?" He finally calls his mom on his portable phone, tells her to look in the inside pocket of his gray suede jacket—and there they are. We all applaud. His mother asks, "What's that noise, where are you?" He doesn't tell her.

Sometimes it works. Sometimes it doesn't. Anne tells us to make sure of the wording of our questions: "Is it raining?" is not enough. "Is it raining on Thirty-fourth Street in New York?" is enough. She says we must accept the first answer—repeatedly asking the question is saying that you didn't like the first answer and you'll just ask till you hear what you want to hear, not what you ought to hear. She warns us not to dowse when we feel tired or ill because then the results will be sloppy.

Larry and I leave early: we *are* tired. We want to think about what we've heard and seen.

On the way home we decide to stop for pizza. Or, rather, we tell each other, if we can find a parking place in front of the restaurant, we'll stop. Otherwise we'll send out.

Nearing our destination, I see that every space is taken. I take out my pendulum, which I've purchased for six dollars from

Anne. In my mind I've already personalized it, as the early dowsers did. Its name is Larry. The two most lovable men I know are Larrys—my own Larry and an editor friend, Larry Ashmead.

"Make there be a parking place in front of Garlic Bob's pizza place," I intone out loud. "We really need this pizza, little pendulum, little Larry, and we want to park our car right *there.*"

Two car lengths ahead of the filled parking space I've targeted, a man gets into his car and pulls out. It'll do.

Parapsychology

Parapsychology (often referred to as "psi") has been defined as the study of any phenomena that cannot be explained by using the normal law of the five senses—although those committed to the subject think that knowledge acquired by other than the usual five senses is very normal indeed. So when one is looking for evidence of psi, one looks for it with a *sixth* sense.

A scientist, for example, can take me into a lab and I easily prove to him that I can recognize a pot roast by the way it looks, feels, tastes, and smells; blindfolded, I can even recognize the scientist by the way he sounds. The pot roast and the scientist are real—my five senses prove it. But unless he tells me either by voice (sound) or body language (sight), I can't know whether the scientist feels hungry for the pot roast or even if he's annoyed with me for bothering him with stupid pot roast–ian experiments. I can't connect with his mind. If I thought I had a sixth sense telling me what the scientist thinks about pot roast and amateur experiments, I couldn't prove it in most scientific laboratories.

In fact, most traditional scientists think parapsychology and a sixth sense are a crock.

"I think traditional science is a crock," says my cousin. "Remember when Dr. Pelner told our moms their arthritis came from dampness? Today's *New York Times* says that scientists find not a shred of evidence linking arthritic pain to dampness, humidity, or any other atmospheric pressures. The same issue of the newspaper," says my cousin, warming to the topic, "reports that science now says there is no possible link between sugar and exuberant behavior in children: all those uneaten candy bars in my house! And," she concludes with a flourish, "last week I noticed the *Jour-*

nal of the American Medical Association giving us the astounding news that low-salt diets don't make us the least bit healthier—although it's been an article of prevailing faith for decades that when it comes to salt, less is better. Right? I'm thinking about throwing out my doctor and trying alternative medicine."

In 1995 the New York Academy of Sciences, alarmed that so many otherwise rational people were buying into alternative medicine and putting as much faith in parapsychology and intuition as they do in their internists, held a conference in New York City entitled "The Flight from Science and Reason": the purpose of the conference was to combat this new, ugly phenomenon—the consideration that there might just be a sixth sense among other ways of knowing things, that there might even be other ways of healing. The scientists called the otherwise rational people "science bashers" and "health quacks" who just loved "bringing the Buddha to work." They called the new interests "antirational and antiscientific." When the "antirationalists" pointed to instances of scientific fraud and said that science is just as fallible as other human endeavors, the scientists at the conference retorted that criticisms like that were "trivial" and that "fraud is an anomaly in science." One scientist blamed it all on the feminists. Another said it was "everybody's job to fight all this antiscientific nonsense."

As Michael Talbot, author of the brilliant *The Holographic Universe,* concludes, "Science is not always as objective as we would like to believe." Talbot thinks we view scientists with too much awe, so that when they proclaim something—like the fact that only five senses exist—we assume it must be true. We forget, says Talbot, "they are only human and subject to the same religious, philosophical, and cultural prejudices as the rest of us." We forget that science tends to change its mind every five minutes or so; remember when they said that chocolate gave you pimples? Remember when going outside with a wet head gave you a cold?

Parapsychology attempts to prove, *in the laboratory*, that there are other ways of knowing things that are different from the way traditional science knows things. For over two thousand years people *have* been reporting odd experiences of knowing something they really couldn't have known or changing something they really couldn't have changed, and for almost as many years, scholars, savants, and forward-thinking scientists have been trying to understand these odd experiences we now refer to as psi. Psychical research has long been written off as the stuff of cranks or frauds, but more and more, says Richard S. Broughton, Ph.D., director of the Rhine Research Center of the Institute for Parapsychology in Durham, North Carolina, people are "beginning to see psi phenomena as extraordinary human abilities; certainly they are poorly understood abilities, but so are many other abilities (like creativity) that we have less problem accepting."

Parapsychologists theorize that we operate at less than 20 percent of our intellectual capacity. To assume that we already know everything there is to know about the mind-body-spirit connection, say parapsychologists, is nothing less than fools' arrogance. In another few decades we'll probably take a sixth sense as much for granted as we do the perceptions of touch or smell. But maybe we'll also be back to believing that dampness causes arthritis.

The Parapsychologists

ESP

If there be a skeptical star I was born under it, Yet I have lived all my days in complete astonishment.

W. MACNEILE DIXON

Dateline: Tokyo. An item in the *San Francisco Examiner* on October 12, 1995, tells us that Sony, the Japanese corporation that revolutionized the world of audio and electronics with such innovations as the Walkman, recently acknowledged what people have been whispering about for years: Sony is indeed conducting research into spoon bending, X-ray vision, telepathy, and other forms of extrasensory perception—or ESP. The Institute of Wisdom was founded in 1989 at the instigation of Sony's founder, Masaru Ibuka, and Akio Morita, its former chairman. The company believes it has already proved the existence of ESP. "Mr. Ibuka and Mr. Morita have long felt there's more to science and technology than what is repeatable, universal, and objective. Some people have the ability to perceive beyond the five senses. This research is intended to investigate how this happens, and why," says a Sony spokesperson.

Tell *that* to your friends who say you're getting really weird with this supernatural stuff.

Of all the paranormal genres, ESP seems to have gained the

most popular support and is considered, by many who have studied or experienced it, to be a *real* thing. That's probably because so many of us have had ESP experiences—whether or not we call it that.

Think of intuition—which is a form of ESP. Have you ever intuitively known who was going to be on the phone as it began to ring? Have you ever "dreamed" someone would have an automobile accident or break a leg or find a wallet—and then, the next day, heard that it happened? Have you ever had a sudden hunch, a bolt from the blue, that helped you solve a problem or make a decision—but there was no apparent logic behind the hunch, only afterward a "How did I think of that" feeling?

You've probably had an ESP moment.

Stephan Fitch is a young New York businessman with a scientific bent, a computer genius, a graduate of the Massachusetts Institute of Technology. He doesn't look or sound like a man who has ESP moments; nevertheless he has them all the time:

I was on my way to dinner at the home of my ex-wife, who is still my good friend, and I felt I wanted to bring her something. Candy? Flowers? Nahhh. Then it came to me in a flash. I wanted to bring her water. Water? Yes. Somehow nothing else would do. Stopping off at a food store, I bought 2 two-gallon jugs of purified water. I'd never done that before—but it just seemed like the right thing.

After opening the package, my ex-wife turned white. "How did you . . . what made you . . . how on earth did you know that my doctor told me not an hour ago that I had a kidney problem and I had to drink enormous amounts of pure water?" she asked.

I just had a feeling, I said.

Don't knock a sixth sense. Don't knock "just a feeling." Don't knock intuition.

• In the late nineteenth century a teenage physics student in Switzerland just has a feeling—a strong sense of himself riding along a light beam. Some years later Albert Einstein offers the world the theory of relativity. Einstein later credited intuition as the source of his finest work, saying, "Intellect has little to do on the road to discovery. There comes a leap in consciousness . . . and the solution seems to come to you, and you don't know why or how."

• In wartime England Winston Churchill is headed for an important meeting, but a gut feeling tells him not to get into the waiting car. He listens to his intuition; a moment later the vehicle explodes.

• Some decades later financial experts tell a Chicago business-man that he'd be insane to follow a feeling in his "funny bone" that directs that he purchase a small chain of hamburger stands; he doesn't listen to the experts, and Ray Kroc fathers McDonald's.

Carl Jung believed that the conscious mind is actually a storing house for the feelings, accumulated memories, wisdom, and experience of the whole human race, and an experience of intuition is only an individual reaching down into that storehouse, a kind of psychic access. No less a scientist than Dr. Paul MacLean, chief of brain evolution and behavior at the National Institutes of Health, says, "Intuition is what the brain knows how to do when you leave it alone . . . it's important to respect the brain's natural ability, to have information coming from your inside world at the same time as things are coming from the outside."

Call it intuition, call it insight, inspiration, or a gut feeling: whatever you want to call it, Stephan Fitch knows he had an ESP moment, connecting with the thoughts of his ex-wife. In her mind she was saying she needed pure water—and he heard it.

The term "ESP" was heard as early as 1892, when Dr. Paul

Joire, a French researcher, observed people who were hypnotized or in a trance and used the term "ESP" to describe their ability to externally sense things without using the known five senses. Have you ever experienced an instantaneous "knowing" about a person or an event without being able to explain how you got the information? Sure you have.

Some of us honor that information; some of us are absolutely uncomfortable with the idea of intuition—it can't be true because I don't remember how I learned it. It's easy to empathize with people who don't trust their ESP; it does threaten logical, linear thinking.

The term "ESP" became popularized in 1930, when Dr. Joseph Banks Rhine created the Duke University laboratory that he headed for three decades. Dr. Rhine was to parapsychology what Freud was to psychoanalysis—a founding father. He and his wife established the scientific foundation for classical laboratory work that statistically proved the existence of ESP and psychokinesis. Rigorous, controlled, repetitive tests helped the parapsychology field lose the notoriety of "occult mysticism." Rhine was one of the first scientists to test for ESP in the laboratory by using decks of playing cards. One of his most famous experiments tested people for their ESP ability by having volunteers try to guess which of five symbols (a cross, a circle, a square, a star, or waves) was on the face of a specially designed "Zener card." After allowing for the number of times the volunteers would guess correctly by pure chance alone, the rate of the volunteers' success that was indisputably beyond pure chance seemed to prove the existence of other "senses" at work. Rhine's work continues at the Institute for Parapsychology in Durham, where experimenters statistically analyze as they rule out "all normal explanations." Respectability was granted to parapsychology by the scientific establishment when, in 1969, the prestigious American Association for the Advancement of Science accepted the Parapsychology Foundation as a member organization—after two previous applications had been rejected.

Rhine's wife, Louisa, also a parapsychologist, determined that ESP "happened" in basically four different forms, most involving some sort of dream. Dreams have always been a common mode for transporting extrasensory information—and no one pretends to know why, although some think that our dreaming minds (even our daydreaming, slightly-in-a-trance minds) don't filter out true extrasensory information that our more "civilized" awake minds resist.

Louisa Rhine believed that *realistic dreams* (those with vivid, detailed imagery of the information conveyed), *unrealistic dreams* (those comprising metaphors and symbols), *hallucinations* (sensory experiences, which include visual and auditory perceptions that relay information), and *intuition* (gut feelings) were responsible for carrying most ESP messages. Today ESP is usually separated into four different categories:

Clairvoyance

Clairvoyance, translated from the French, means "clear seeing": the "seeing" applies to either internal or external visions or even a sensing of images. People who have clairvoyance can sense information about the physical world with something beyond the five. Spatial distance or physical shielding have no effect on clairvoyance. Classical card tests in parapsychology laboratories reveal that there are those who can tell the order of a deck of cards when no living human knows what the order is. Many studies show enough hits to establish something other than chance—in other words, clairvoyance.

Dr. Rhine even tested for animal clairvoyance at Duke, and he claims to have found animals who could sense the impending return of a master and impending danger or death to themselves or to beloved humans. He also tested for animals' ability to "see" their way home even when thousands of miles away in alien territory.

Different types of human clairvoyance have been tested, including

- *X-ray clairvoyance:* the ability to see through opaque objects.
- *Medical clairvoyance:* the ability to see disease in others—even from very far away. Edgar Cayce was a famous medical clairvoyant who not only saw, but correctly diagnosed and prescribed for very distant patients—and he never had a moment's medical training.
- *Traveling clairvoyance:* the ability to see activities, people, and objects that are very far removed from the subject.
- *Spatial clairvoyance:* the ability to have visions that transcend place and time—the kind psychics claim to have.
- *Dream clairvoyance:* the ability to dream of an event that is happening at the same time you dream it.
- *Spiritual clairvoyance:* the ability to have visions of "angelic" beings—popularized recently in many books about angels.

T e l e p a t h y

This is another form of ESP, also hotly debated among traditional scientists and parapsychologists. It originates from the Greek term *tele* ("distant") and *pathe* ("feeling"), and it simply connotes mind-to-mind communication by means other than the five senses. The usual laboratory experiments involved one person in a room looking at one card after another from a thoroughly shuffled deck while a "receiver" in another room wrote down impressions of the cards being looked at. Today more sophisticated (and interesting) laboratory tests are available—as I discovered. More "hits" than can reasonably be expected to occur by chance establish telepathic skills.

Sigmund Freud recognized telepathy because it occurred so often in his practice; he finally termed it a regressive, primitive faculty lost through human evolution, but one that could return under certain circumstances. Carl Jung considered telepathy a function of synchronicity (coincidences that may be more than just chance), and that will be discussed further on in this chapter.

Research has indicated that telepathy seems to be tied to emotions—both of the sender and the receiver. It occurs most often in situations of crisis when one becomes aware of danger to another who is far away. Interestingly, it has been measured biologically: blood volume changes and electroencephalogram monitors show that recipients' brain waves change to match those of the sender! In 1971 astronaut Edgar D. Mitchell aboard *Apollo 14* was chosen to conduct a telepathy experiment with four receivers on earth, 150,000 miles below his spacecraft. Mitchell concentrated on sequences of twenty-five random numbers and completed two hundred sequences. Guessing forty correctly would be pure chance. Two recipients scored significantly higher.

Mitchell's Soviet counterpart, cosmonaut Vitaly Sevastyanov, says that while in space, he was able to mentally signal his fellow cosmonaut when he wanted a tool. The other cosmonaut would then hand it to him—no words having passed between them.

Precognition

This is yet another form of ESP, and it suggests *knowing the future* through means other than the five senses.

The classic laboratory test for precognition is to ask a subject to predict the order of a deck of cards that will be shuffled thoroughly sometime in the future.

Of all nonlaboratory ESP experiences, this is the most frequently reported—usually within one or two days of the future event—and it often involves a severe emotional shock. By four to one, most precognition concerns illness, death, dying, or natural disasters, and usually, close friends or relatives seem to be involved. One theory of precognition holds that having the mental experience unleashes a powerful energy called "psychokinesis," which then actually causes the envisioned future to happen. Most believers will say that few people can actually foresee their own death—probably because the mind rejects such horror. There are always exceptions—like Abraham Lincoln, who dreamed of his own death six weeks before the event, and John Garfield and William McKinley, who also foresaw their own violent ends.

Psychokinesis (or PK)

The final commonly studied element of ESP is psychokinesis— the purported ability to influence people's actions from a distance or move or change inanimate objects purely by mental power—in other words, mind over matter.

This is the way PK usually works: Someone wishes for, then concentrates hard on, a physical result—and it happens.

The term stems from the Greek word *psyche* ("breath," "life," or "soul") and *kinein* ("to move"). Traditionally it has been thought to be both an unconscious or conscious process, and it has been observed since ancient times in levitations, miraculous psychic healings, breaking or bending of objects, influencing dice to fall in a certain way, and other physical phenomena. The classic testing device for PK has been thrown dice (often tossed by a machine), as the person throwing the dice tries to influence the fall by wishing it to go a certain way. The results have usually been statistically significant in favor of PK.

Experiments in psychic healing—concentrating on changing a condition in the human body—have been done by, in particular,

Bernard Grad, a biologist with the Alan Memorial Institute of McGill University in Montreal, Canada, and William Braud, a psychologist working at the Mind Science Foundation in San Antonio, Texas. Grad found that mice, simply touched by a "healer," showed significantly faster wound healing than mice who were not touched. Braud has shown important results in studies involving biofeedback (a form of PK), where subjects control the activities within their own bodies—for example, heart rate, blood pressure, brain waves, and skin temperature—simply by the use of various mental exercises. Biofeedback is used in some of the world's most modern rehabilitation centers, including the Rusk Institute in New York City. Braud's most recent research involves outsiders who, by their own mental concentration, are able to influence someone else's physiology!

Research in the field grows at a strong rate—probably influenced by the public exposure to performance artists like Israeli psychic Uri Geller, who apparently can bend spoons through his concentration and a few soft taps of his fingers; his powers are said to be so intense that some viewers, watching him on television, noticed their own spoons undergoing similar changes. Although his critics are legion, no one has yet been able to prove that Geller uses sleight of hand or other magician-type effects to fool his audiences.

These four, then—clairvoyance, telepathy, precognition, and psychokinesis—constitute psi, or parapsychology, as it's practiced today.

It's fascinating to note that in December of 1995 the media reported that the CIA recommended suspending a top-secret parapsychology program called Stargate that it had been quietly funding to the tune of $20 million since the seventies, when reports leaked that the Soviets were engaged in psychokinesis experiments as well as remote viewing (visualizing an adversary from a distance to see what he's doing). Did Stargate work—and why haven't we heard more about it?

Edwin May, a nuclear physicist who ran Stargate for ten years at California's Stanford Research Institute (SRI) and the Science Applications International Corporation (SAIC) in Silicon Valley, talking about remote viewing experiments, said in an interview with Ted Koppel on *Nightline* that "fifteen percent of the data was of such quality that it could have been sketched." As an example, he cited drawings of an underground nuclear test site in the Soviet Union that had been done by a remote viewer and later corroborated by other sources. Ingo Swann, a remote viewing participant in Stargate for sixteen years, said the 15 percent figure was actually low because it represented "only the baseline that ordinary nongifted and untrained persons often achieve." Swann said ESP is latent in almost everyone, and those who were ultimately chosen for the program and subsequently trained had a success rate that reached as high as 65 percent!

RICHARD S. BROUGHTON, PH.D., AND CHERYL ALEXANDER

Larry and I are in Durham, North Carolina—about to take part in psi—specifically, an ESP experiment called the autoganzfeld, affectionately known as the ganzfeld to the researchers who know and love it.

In 1962 Dr. J. B. Rhine, founder of the Duke University Parapsychology Laboratory, determined that research in the still controversial field of parapsychology needed to be independent of the pressures of academic politics. With the help of old benefactors who had supported Duke's efforts and new benefactors who believed in the need for an independent, international organization, Rhine founded the Foundation for Research on the Nature of Man (in 1995 renamed the Rhine Research Center in his honor). He determined it would follow the scientific quest wherever it might lead.

This is exactly where Larry and I are about to undergo some personal experimentation. We're shown around the Rhine Center by its executive director, Sally Rhine Feather, Ph.D., daughter of Dr. Rhine. She has a huge responsibility, she tells us, because lack of funding for parapsychology has closed down most of the other organizations devoted to the scientific investigation of the unknown capabilities of the human mind, capabilities suggesting that consciousness can interact with the physical world in ways not yet recognized by science. Despite all this nonrecognition from the traditional scientific world, a recent *Newsweek* cover announces that AMERICA IS HOOKED ON THE PARANORMAL, and surveys show that anywhere from one-half to three-quarters of the population say they've had experiences they believe are telepathic. So what do you do with all these Americans and their convictions? Ignore them? No. They're the reason Dr. Rhine and her associates are passionately committed to conducting first-class research in the areas of extrasensory perception—telepathy, clairvoyance, precognition, and psychokinesis.

So that's what drew me to Durham: I wanted to find a place where science was going on—not just belief.

The most important intellectual tool of the institute's scientists—of any scientist—is "critical doubt," says director Richard S. Broughton, Ph.D., author of *Parapsychology: The Controversial Science,* and my kind of guy. He distinguishes a healthy skepticism from a corrosive skepticism. His work—and the work of other parapsychologists who gather here regularly to share experiments and insights? To confront the anomalies of nature that seem most connected to the human mind.

However, "even critical doubt can go too far," notes Broughton. "Today, many scientists choose to deal with anomalies by denying their existence . . . even when they can't deny the experiences or observations that underlie the anomaly." So my husband and I volunteer as guinea pigs for one of these anomalies—ESP. Dr. Broughton will oversee it.

The only thing I know about extrasensory perception is that almost everyone is said to have this sixth sense; some have developed it more than others. The evidence seems to be strong that ESP is inherited and people born with striking evidence of ESP gifts seem to come in families. If one has a highly developed sixth sense, she's supposed to be able to receive information about the present, past, and future through means beyond touch, taste, hearing, sight, and smell. This information usually comes in the form of "gut feelings," dreams, and premonitions. One theory holds that ESP has been around forever—that it's a primordial sense with which people have lost touch as civilization and technology progresses. Another theory holds that ESP is a supersense that's just evolving in the nervous system.

But where exactly does this sixth sense, ESP, reside in the human? Is there a kind of brain geography? Can it be pointed to in the left or right hemisphere? If the sixth sense does not reside in the brain, does it squat in the belly button, hide in the foot or the genitals? Maybe I'll find out here.

The experiment Larry and I are part of is one of a new and special series involving "emotionally close" participants—siblings, parent-child pairs, or happily married couples. The institute has had uncommon success in its general ESP experiments; emotionally close subjects may be an important variable and one that is just starting to be tested. Researchers are hopeful that results in this area will be significant.

It comes down to this: Will I be able to "hear" what Larry is thinking? Can he send me his thoughts if he tries really hard? I mean—we're definitely emotionally close, having had a swell marriage for over thirty years. And there have been certain signs that I can almost read his mind, feel in my gut when he's reaching out to me—signs that he, by the way, cheerfully discounts. I, on the other hand, take them quite for granted. For example: As a journalist working at home, my telephone rings at least thirty times a day. When Larry is the one who's calling, *I always know it before I pick up the receiver.* I don't know how I know—I just do. I've thought of the possible explanations—and none holds water. I mean, he calls at different hours during the day, so it's not that I anticipate his call at a certain time. I truly know when it's he on the phone when it rings. Believe it. And I also seem to know when he's in trouble—although this is not as well documented as the phone calls. For example, one day last summer I *knew* there was a problem. He was out on his beloved boat, and I was home alone in New York and a wreck. Now, Larry is always out on that boat and it's a fact of our lives, but this day just seemed to be different. I had angst in my heart. I called my son, I called the bait guy at the marina, I called the Coast Guard for the latest weather report—in one way or another, everyone told me I was nuts to worry. The day was gorgeous, and he was probably knocking them dead in the bluefish department.

But I wasn't nuts to worry. The day dragged on, and Larry's on-time arrival at the dock didn't happen (I was calling the marina every twenty minutes). Naturally it didn't happen. The boat had sprung a leak twenty miles out to sea, and Larry and his crew, bailing furiously, managed to make it home—four hours past the time he was due. Forget the infuriating fact that my husband could have given the Coast Guard an SOS over his boat radio but didn't because he has a hard time asking for boating assistance.

Still, he really didn't have to SOS the Coast Guard: he'd sent a mental message to me. Believe it. Nevertheless, in another half hour *I* would have set the Coast Guard and maybe the United States Marines on his trail.

So stuff like this goes on all the time.

We are greeted before the experiment by a young, blond, Rapunzel-haired Cheryl Alexander, one of the very pleasant ganzfeld researchers. An interjection here: None of the parapsychology scientists I'm to meet will look like "crazies"—something I'd expected, I'm embarrassed to admit—not *one* wild-haired, loony-eyed Mel Brooks type in the lot at the Rhine Research Center. Actually, most looked like me and Larry and my professor cousin. We give Cheryl the long information forms we've filled out—forms on which we've described our habits, our background, the things we love, and the things we hate like poison. Later the scientists will feed this information into a computer for the purposes of analyzing the subjects and their rates of success and failure. The goal of the forms is to reach a predictive point where scientists eventually can say that a person with certain traits and interests will do best in a specific type of ESP experiment.

Cheryl asks which of us will "receive" and which of us will send the message. No problem deciding: I'll receive. I always receive. She shows us the room where Larry will be comfortably seated. There on a television screen, she explains, he will see a scene that will be repeated several times. The scene has been selected randomly by a computer from a bank of about two hundred images; no one, not even Cheryl, knows which images will appear on Larry's screen. For thirty minutes he's to concentrate on that scene on his television screen. He's instructed to describe it out loud, write on a pad, use any method he can think of to mentally send to my mind a picture of what he's seeing on the screen.

Then she leads us both to the room I'll occupy. Center stage is a comfortable, leather reclining chair with blankets piled nearby for my comfort. I will, says Cheryl, be asked to cover my eyes with halved Ping-Pong balls, which, in turn, are held in place by goggles. I am instructed to keep my eyes open as much as possible, and what I'll be seeing is pink—just a stretch of pink created by two overhead one-hundred-watt, red flood lamps that will shine down on my covered eyes. I'll be totally alone with the light, my entire visual field cut down to the uniform pink blur. The purpose of this technique, I'm told, is to place me in a mild state of sensory deprivation with no pattern or detail to distract me.

Why is all this preparation necessary? If ESP is, as many scientists believe, a different but weaker sense form, it might be overwhelmed by the conventional strong signals constantly assailing us. The optimal state for receiving extrasensory signals is described by some as "almost sleep"—a very loose, relaxed, daydreamy state of mind. The aim, then, is to reduce all distractions to the receiver and the sender of images—both of whom are instructed to try to make their minds almost blank.

What next? I'm to be further cut off from outside distractions by a "white noise" that will be piped into my room—a kind of hiss that sounds like waves breaking in the surf; this will mask any outside sound. Then, Cheryl says, I'm to talk out loud about any images that pass through my mind, no matter how bizarre, no matter how commonplace. Talk to myself? Well, not really, because my voice will be piped into the room where Larry is looking at the image on the television screen and into the room where she will be sitting monitoring both of us on a closed-circuit television.

Both Larry and I will be able to hear Cheryl give us directions; she will tape and also take written notes of everything Larry and I each say in the privacy of our respective rooms.

We settle in. Cheryl helps me don the halved Ping-Pong balls and the goggles. I can't hear what's happening in Larry's room, but, stretched out in the recliner, snuggled under the blanket, shoes off, and masked, I feel warm and cocooned; the only thing I can see is that soft, rose glow.

Cheryl starts a tape before the actual experiment starts; it's a fifteen-minute series of relaxation exercises recited by a woman with a low, hypnotic voice. This is corny, I think. The voice instructs me to let go mentally, not even try to concentrate on the image Larry is supposed to be sending. All I'm to do, right now, is feel my arms and legs go heavy, feel my breathing slow. I do. I must admit, though, I'm conscious of watching myself try to relax, because I know very well I'll be describing the experience later, in this book. And that's a tad offputting. I mean, I can't *totally* relax, but then again, can anyone? And I'm a bit suspicious: is it possible I'm being hypnotized? It won't work. Others have tried. Well, so what if it *does* work? I reason. If someone can hypnotize me to receive an unseen image, that alone proves something.

I decide that this is not the right attitude, and I try to lose myself in the voice. After fifteen minutes I'm a torpid lump in the chair. The relaxation tape stops and Cheryl's voice asks me if I'm all right. Yes, I say. She tells me that next I'm to free-associate— talk about whatever comes into my mind, describe any image I see behind the rosy glow, talktalktalk to the empty room. Cheryl will give me a copy of what I've said, after the experiment.

The white noise starts. I hear surf and see pink, and then, although I feel stupid doing it, in about five minutes I do start to talk. And I say:

I see dolphins jumping—many dolphins making a U-shaped arc in the air. Rounded shapes, now, and a parachute opening and puffs of smoke. And crows—like that Van Gogh painting, thousands of V-shaped crows. There's sea foam rising, waves, waves, puffs of smoke rising over the waves, blue and gray. Wait—now here's a house in Ireland, peat roofs, white puffs, mushroom-shaped clouds, parachutes, the dolphins again—rise and fall of the jump of the dolphins. A moor like in Jane Eyre. *Those parachutes are wafting about.*

For half an hour I talk like this to the empty room, letting the images flow, free-associating, describing what I see under the Ping-Pong ball mask. I can just visualize Larry concentrating, concentrating, trying to send me his thoughts. Oh, I hope they're of dolphins and moors. C'*mon*, Larry!

Finally the white noise stops. Cheryl's voice instructs me to remove the goggles and the Ping-Pong balls. I do—and slowly adjust to the light. On a television screen in front of me, Cheryl says, four picture scenes will appear, one by one. She directs me to pick up a knoblike control on the nearby table and rate each of the four scenes according to the similarity they have to my imaginings. One of the pictures will be the one Larry has been trying to send to me.

The first scene is of ballet dancers. I start to talk, again:

It's possible, just possible, that the V of the uplifted arms and the V the legs of the dancers make is similar to the flowing van Gogh crows I saw, the black V-shaped crows. Maybe, maybe, this is what Larry saw, too. But I think I'm stretching it. Nahh—this is not right.

With my knob I rate the dancers a five, giving credit for the V's. The scene recedes from the television set, and the next comes on. Now I am jolted upright into my chair.

There it is—the parachutes! the puffs of smoke! *I recognize it, I do! There's a helicopter battle, and I didn't see that at all, but Cheryl—there are the rounded shapes in the background. Sure, they're mountains, not dolphins, but still—I saw that roundness, the puffs,* and those parachutes!!

I rate the helicopter battle a nine, and I'm sure I've got it.

The next scene comes on. It is of Richard Burton making a speech. He's wearing a tall white miter on his head—he is obviously a bishop—and he seems to be excommunicating someone.

I love Richard Burton, but nothing. There is nothing in this scene that is even vaguely familiar.

I rate it a zero.

The last image comes on. It is of giant iguanas.

Well, there's the moor behind the iguanas, the landscape seems familiar . . . but iguanas? No. Nope. This is not right.

I give the iguanas a three.

Cheryl tells me that the experiment is over. She's going to show me the images that Larry saw—the ones he was sending me. I can hardly wait.

They both come in—Larry is grinning. She does something to the television and here comes the scene that Larry has been trying to send me via ESP.

Richard Burton.

Oh no.

We've flubbed miserably. Failed at ESP. Failed the worst we could fail. Richard Burton? God damn it.

Larry tells me that he could hear me saying "mushroom clouds . . . parachutes . . . V shapes . . ."

"No, no—no mushrooms. No parachutes. No miserable moors," he was yelling in frustration. "Richard Burton. Richard Burton!! White robe, miter, Richard Burton . . . stop with the puffs of smoke!"

To no avail.

Well, thank God we can communicate verbally, says Larry in consolation. I guess he's right, but I wanted to have extrasensory talents, also. And I don't.

It doesn't mean that, says Cheryl.

So what *does* it mean?

It means, says Cheryl, that you're either having a bad day ESP-wise or that Larry and you seem to exhibit psychic ability on the ganzfeld less readily than others might. In another setting you might exhibit much stronger psychic talents.

Dr. Richard Broughton, the tall, bearded, wry director of the institute, says that "parapsychologists simply do not have any means of measuring 'raw' psychic ability. Everything we've learned so far indicates that psychic ability is not under conscious control. Thus, how psychic ability is used by the subject probably depends very heavily on the situation in which he or she is asked to use it."

But wait! I *did* see the parachutes and the puffs of smoke of the helicopter battle—what was that all about?

Cheryl's not too impressed, although, she allows, maybe some precognition was working here—my ability to see into the future, what was *going* to be on the screen. But we weren't testing for that, there were no controls for that, so we can't lend it too much credence.

I persist. What's the odds of seeing parachutes and smoke puffs just before I'm shown a scene with parachutes and smoke puffs? I demand to know. Probably very low, Cheryl concedes.

All right, all right. Forget it.

Here's an interesting postscript:

The ganzfeld-ESP experiments at the Rhine Institute for Parapsychology in general (and no thanks to me) have enjoyed significant critical success: that is, the researchers have achieved statistically significant scoring rates—much higher than success rates that can be attributed to mere chance. By chance alone, a receiver of another's thoughts should score a hit one time in four for a 25 percent success rate. In a 1985 analysis of twenty-eight ESP studies from several labs, the late Charles Honorton, of the University of Edinburgh, calculated a combined hit rate of 35 percent. A run of 354 sessions reported in 1994 by Honorton yielded 32 percent. And, even more remarkable, a recent run at Edinburgh, using art students (are they more 'sensitive'?) got nearly a 50 percent hit rate! These extraordinary rates of success confirm the results of the Rhine Institute. There's something going on here—even though you couldn't prove it by me.

Still, I leave, feeling more mollified with our results. In a 1995 scientific abstract, the institute reports that in the experiments for "emotionally close" subjects, parent-child and sibling subjects scored much higher for ESP than did the husband-and-wife subjects.

"Comment on the correlations observed so far must remain extremely tentative," note researchers Broughton and Alexander.

So we flunked extrasensory perception. Be that as it may, *I will still* follow my gut instincts when Larry's too long at sea. And I'll feel comfortable answering the phone, "Hello, honey," when I feel he's on the other end.

Synchronicity

> *A coincidence! The odds are enormous against its being a coincidence. No figures could express them. No, my dear Watson, the two events are connected—must be connected. It is for us to find the connection.*
>
> SHERLOCK HOLMES,
> "THE ADVENTURE OF THE SECOND STAIN"

For as long as she could remember, she and her mom had gotten on each other's nerves. The mother was so judgmental, always nagging, always criticizing. Some weeks ago she decided to drive home to see her mother for the weekend, hoping against hope that the two days would be wonderful. They weren't. They were murder.

They constantly missed the boat, argued incessantly, and driving away, the young woman knew the visit had taken a particularly heavy toll on her heart. She felt numb. Why hadn't her mom ever loved her? Why was she so critical? After arriving home, she flung herself on the bed and sobbed. Her body was racked with sorrow—she just couldn't stop crying.

Suddenly a loud slam of noise startled her, and she jumped a mile! What was that? *A book had escaped from its place on a shelf filled with twenty other books and fallen to the floor. She picked it up and glanced at the title.*

It was My Mother, My Self *by Nancy Friday. Someone had given it to her years before, but she'd never touched it. The hair on the back of her neck stood up. Now she read nonstop until she'd finished the book.*

Finally she understood that the things her mother did that she'd interpreted as unloving were actually coming from a place of pure love and anxiety for her daughter. Underneath the mother's carping was her tremendous wish for her child's happiness.

The book transformed their relationship. The young woman stopped being guarded with her mother, let her love show, and let her mom's love in.

What happened here? Why did the book fall from the shelf in my friend Susan's home? Why *that* book? Pure coincidence? Or was the falling book somehow meant to happen?

Was it synchronicity?

Looking for the sixth sense requires that attention be paid to the phenomenon known as synchronicity, which was defined by Carl Jung as coincidences that are so unusual and meaningful, they can't be attributed to chance alone. They are beyond coincidence. Some say that when these fabulous coincidences occur—the book falling from the shelf, the lovers who discover that the father of one and the mother of the other had also been in love thirty-five years before, the writer who, on the street, bumps into the reclusive subject of her next article—maybe we should look at them as evidence that life is filled with meaning and mystery and that we have extraordinary, unused power from senses we don't even know exist.

After all, why is it we *"just happen"* to meet the people we meet just when we *need* to meet them? Why is it we find the article on Rome just when we've been thinking about going to Rome? Why is it that Christopher Reeve portrayed a paralyzed cop in a movie—actually learned how to *be* a paralyzed person—*just* before the riding accident that paralyzed him?

Is it possible there's a sort of universal plan behind all these "accidental coincidences" and we ourselves are, in part, the planners? Is it possible that these coincidences may be a sign that there's a higher intelligence at work, a kind of poetry to the universe? Is it possible that a sixth sense dictates these synchronicities?

Jung believed that many of his patients' ideas bubbled up from a level deeper than any one patient's mind: they came, thought Jung, from the collective memory of the human race itself—as if each of us has the memory of a two-million-year-old person hiding out in our subconscious minds. He was convinced that thoughts and emotions deep in a person's psyche could literally affect events happening in the world today.

There was, believed the analyst, an interconnectedness among *all* things in the universe, and it was synchronicity—these very meaningful coincidences—that linked the material world (the one made up of physical matter) to the psychic world (the one that pertains to the human soul or mind).

The experience that started Jung thinking about synchronicity occurred while he was treating a woman whose logical, controlled way of thinking was blocking her therapy. One day she happened to tell Jung about her dream, in which she was given a costly piece of jewelry in the form of a golden scarab beetle. The scarab was an image used among ancient Egyptians as a symbol representing rebirth, and the analyst wondered to himself if the woman's unconscious mind was announcing that she was going to undergo a psychological rebirth. As he opened his mouth to tell her this theory, he looked up to see a rare, golden green scarab beetle tapping gently against the other side of his window—the only time he'd ever seen one there. Jung knew it was strange for an insect to attempt to enter a dark room from the bright daylight; he immediately opened the window, caught the insect as it flew in, and handed the beetle to his patient with the words "Here is your scarab."

When the beetle entered the room at the moment she was telling her scarab dream, Jung's patient was deeply moved. This healing and transforming experience allowed her to make a breakthrough—to cast off her rigidity and flow with her analysis.

The question: Did either Jung or his patient somehow unconsciously produce that scarab to affect a change in the patient's analysis? Did either the patient or the analyst open up to something beyond the five senses to make that remarkable synchronicity occur? Or was it simply pure chance that a rare scarab flew into the treatment room as a difficult patient was describing a dream about a scarab? It would be easy to attribute it to pure chance, but it probably would be wrong.

Surely there have always been synchronistic events, but now, more than three decades after Jung's death, *quantum physics* offers scientific evidence for synchronicity. This new and sometimes controversial genre of physics began with Einstein's theory of relativity, in which Einstein posited that space and time are not separate entities, but are linked and part of a larger whole he called the space-time continuum.

University of London physicist David Bohm, Einstein's protégé and one of the world's most respected quantum physicists, took this idea a giant step further. He says that *everything* in the universe is part of a continuum. Bohm believes that despite the apparent separateness of things, everything is a seamless extension of everything else. For example, says Michael Talbot, author of *The Holographic Universe,* imagine that the light streaming from the lamp beside you, the dog at your feet, your hand, are not merely *made* of the same thing, they *are* the same thing—one unbroken, enormous something that's extended "uncountable arms and appendages into all the apparent objects, atoms, restless oceans, and twinkling stars in the cosmos." Still, David Bohm doesn't believe the universe is a giant, amorphous mass; he says things can be part of an undivided whole and still retain their unique qualities. The drops of water, the little pools and drafts that often form in a river, possess individual characteristics of size, depth, and direction of flow, but even looking very carefully, we cannot tell where any given little pool ends and where the river begins.

Many traditional scientists on the cutting edge of the coming millennium also agree that we're all linked, that there's matter and there is space and both interact. Indeed, we are wonderfully connected and bound together by gravitational and even electromagnetic interaction; there really is a web in which we're all caught together. Every atom in our bodies is drawn down toward the earth and toward each other. No one has yet been able definitely to correlate the significance of all this, but gravitational connections certainly exist.

"And can we connect electromagnetically?" asks physicist Eugene Hecht. "The air force already has a program where they're able to read brain waves and feed them into computers; an individual can put on a little helmet, think thoughts, and the helmet will pick up electromagnetic signals sent by the currents in the brain and translate them into words—albeit on a very elementary level. But, in fifty years, will I be able to put on a little helmet and read someone else's mind and will he be able to read mine? Yes."

Jung applied the term "synchronicity" to J. B. Rhine's ESP card-guessing experiments at Duke University, and synchronicity is increasingly coming to light in the modern research of psychologists, parapsychologists, and scientists who study the nature of consciousness.

Think of it this way: If anyone had told a citizen of the American Revolution that radio and television waves would eventually connect everyone in the universe and that I would even be able to capture his very voice in a little box and play it back to myself later—would he not have also scoffed? If ESP is already possible through electromagnetic energy interactions, is it such a leap to believe that energy waves can connect us synchronistically to other people and other forces? As Sam Keen, spiritual seeker, leader of the new men's movement, and author of *Hymns to an Unknown God* notes, "A marriage is in the making between physics and mysticism. Quantum physics has demonstrated the limits of the old, time-bound, space-bound Newtonian materialistic universe of isolated atoms."

"What I *know,*" says Keen, "is that synchronicity *doesn't* happen to anybody who thinks the universe is nothing but a set of rules. Even if eighty percent of our lives unfold in a rule-governed universe, twenty percent says we interact in ways for which we have absolutely no paradigms. Synchronicities will never occur to those who have only one explanation for how things happen, who don't understand that we really don't *know* how the human spirit interacts with the world.

"At the gut level," continues Keen, "what we all ultimately want to know is if the universe is addressing *me,* not human beings in general. *Me. My* life. Having a synchronistic experience is like the universe suddenly saying, 'Sam Keen, are you there?' Not 'To Whom It May Concern, are you there?' "

Keen tells a story:

"I went to school with a woman named Jane Haynes, and we were sweethearts but rather too much for each other, so she went off and married a marine and I married someone else and later got divorced. She went to live in Monterey and we lost touch, but many years later I happened to be in California and thought, Maybe I'll just see if old Jane is around. But I didn't call her.

"Later, on the highway, on my way home, I had the same thought and a few hours to kill, so this time I stopped at a toll-booth phone to call her, but she wasn't home.

"I opened the door of the phone booth to leave, and there she was, walking toward me on the highway. Old Jane. Walking toward me. Her car had broken down.

"It was important to me to see Jane again," says Keen. "See, the universe was talking to me.

"We get embarrassed in this world because we don't know why unexplainable things happen. So we use words like 'chance' or 'happenstance.' That throws a blanket over philosophical waters and doesn't tell you a damn thing. It's *synchronicity* that paints a bridge over the chasm and tells us that the world works in ways more mysterious than the human mind can ever comprehend."

Deepak Chopra, M.D., the mind/body guru and author of many books on how to connect to our inner selves, believes that mostly untapped energies bring about synchronistic events. Chopra is a medical doctor, and I asked him how a scientific mind can buy into synchronicity and forces beyond the five senses.

"If you really understand what science is telling us," replies Dr. Chopra, "it's that the essential nature of the world is made up of information *and* energy. If the world were just material, we wouldn't be speaking to each other on the phone, we wouldn't have fax machines or computers.

"The spirit," continues Chopra, "is a real force of energy, just like gravity is a real force; and the spirit is that domain of our awareness where we connect with everything else. Connecting takes *intention,* though, and I believe that you can actually induce a synchronistic happening to occur when you introduce an *intention* at a subtle level of consciousness. When you learn to do this spontaneously, you enter a state of grace where, more and more, you experience meaningful coincidences."

Dan Wakefield, journalist, novelist, and screenwriter, agrees with Chopra that we can create synchronicity. We need to allow for miracles, for the truly mystical coincidences that are more than chance. A couple of years ago Wakefield was down on his luck. Problems from alcoholism and writer's block had him "running on empty in terms of cash as well as ideas. I need a miracle," he told a friend. Those were his exact words. Three days later he got a call from Harper/San Francisco, a publisher with whom he'd never done business, asking him to write a book.

"What's it about?" asked Wakefield.

"Miracles," he was told. Wakefield, now the author of *Expect a Miracle,* believes in synchronicity with all his heart. He says that some people have learned actually to create an atmosphere in which synchronicity more easily occurs; to these people, miraculous coincidences seem to happen *all the time.* "They are open to possibility," says Wakefield, "awake to their own consciousness. They know how to tune *out* the stuff that distracts—like alcohol, drugs, Walkman players, and the fifty-five television channels available for surfing. A mind that is open to synchronistic connections is just going to see more in the world than can be explained in a textbook."

It's true: some people rely on their sixth sense more than others and hardly even notice it. These are the people who seem always to have an intuitive way of knowing things. These are the people who strongly feel connection to others and to the universe at a profound level. These are the people who notice synchronicities occurring around them almost every day.

Other people, logical, very rational people, even when pressed, can't think of ever experiencing a single meaningful coincidence.

As for me, I have to admit something: the more I think about synchronicity, the more I experience it, the more I'm sure it's a real thing. I feel eerie connections between the things I'm working on and what's happening *inside* me and what's happening in the outer world. Perhaps it's a case of the ancient Chinese saying "When the pupil is ready, the teacher will come."

Philosopher Gary Zukav, author of *The Seat of the Soul,* has an interesting take on synchronicity. Do not insist, he says, "that the universe comply with your understanding of it. Don't you think it's arrogant to imagine that the universe operates as we think it should?" he asks.

Yes. If some great universal consciousness does exist, it operates with the seamlessness of a miracle, as Wakefield thinks, not according to person-made parameters. And in order to be ready for remarkable, unpredictable occurrences, Zukav suggests we become "multisensory" instead of five-sensory humans. The multisensory human, says Zukav, has perceptions that extend beyond physical reality into an "invisible realm" where intuition, hunches, and subtle feelings have as much validity as physical realities. The synchronicities that will occur to a multisensory person, says Zukav, are "an occasional glimpse into the exquisite awesomeness of life. Trust it. Celebrate it when it happens."

I trust it.

And you have to trust me. What I'm about to tell you, happened. It isn't an exaggeration, it isn't a joke.

Driving home in my sporty Saab convertible from a visit to friends at Candlewood Lake, I was thinking about two things. One was synchronicity. *Can* forces beyond the five senses create remarkable coincidences? I was wondering how I'd end this section on synchronicity.

The other thing I was thinking about was my finger. Helping my host, Roz, I'd sliced the cucumbers for dinner, and a nice chunk of finger along with the cukes. Now the Band-Aid had fallen off, and my finger was really burning. I was thinking how I wished I had another Band-Aid.

One flew into the car. Flew *into* the car. A Band-Aid.

I put it on.

So?

MY MOM WAS NOT AN OPEN-MINDED WOMAN.

She was funny and smart and fiercely loyal, but I have to be honest: her favorite saying was a disapproving "It's a whole new world" whenever she was faced with sexual mores, electrical equipment, or parental issues her mother never had to face. It wasn't her world, and she never tried to make it hers. My mom missed out.

I'm not going to miss out. The fact is, I no longer want to live in an echo chamber of my own circular thoughts. I am my mother's child, I always will be, but it's not written in stone that I have to share her distrust of the unknown, even though I'm not sanguine about ever finding the Internet. I've spent two years now looking for Mom and me—and I feel satisfied that I've found some answers—although not, in some cases, the ones I sought. I hope that the psychic Rosemary Altea was correct when she told me my darling mom has been enlightened. Because *I've* been enlightened.

I think I'm enlightened because I'm now convinced, for example, there's synchronicity. And intuition. And people who are so exquisitely sensitive that they really seem to be able to tap into other worlds. Writing this book has forced me to consider the possibility that maybe, just maybe, there *are* other senses that even

I own—senses that can't be explained by the current, scientific worldview. Perhaps there *is* a sixth sense that somehow can work as reliably as the other five—and perhaps there's even a seventh or eighth sense, though most twentieth-century scientists would fight me to the death on that one.

I'm not sure about disciplines like dowsing, but I still can't explain how I dowsed up that parking space.

It's shortsighted to be closed-minded. I'll probably always have problems with the ET and the X-Files hypotheses, but now I'm willing to at least entertain the idea that I can't see the forest for the trees. Or, as William Irwin Thompson put it, "We are like flies crawling across the ceiling of the Sistine Chapel: we cannot see what angels or gods lie underneath the threshold of our perceptions."

Since starting this book, I've also become convinced that the universe talks to me—Sherry—not to 'To Whom It May Concern." And whose little voice was that ringing in my ears right before I went on television last week, saying quietly, "Wear the pearls"? Was it merely a memory of my mom? A metaphor of my mom? I don't *think* so.

Look—I've decided this: I can still be me, still be my own questioning self, and at the same time listen hungrily to an astrologist without being sure he's out to fool me. I want the *chance* of otherworldliness in my life. The best part: I refuse to be self-conscious about my new explorations.

The bottom line is this: As the faithful trumpet the glories of the paranormal and the scholars debunk them, there's you and me left to try them. You and me left, perhaps to be amazed that we can do what we previously knew was impossible. You and me left to wonder that maybe, maybe, in some fabulous way, we are connected to the past, to the future, and to the spirit of each other. St.

Augustine said, "Miracles do not happen in contradiction of nature, but in contradiction to what we know about nature."

St. Augustine aside, I think it was no miracle but, instead, this uncommon voyage that allowed me to stop feeling furious at my mom for her mothering that sometimes went wrong. I think that reaching out to her through the supernatural helped me to stop holding her responsible for my shortcomings. I will no longer blame her totally for my fear of risk taking, for my controlling personality, for my deep-seated terror of being *ordinary,* for the failures of my own mothering. (I'll only blame her a little.)

So maybe I didn't *really* get to another lifetime, and maybe it wasn't *really* my mother who, through the medium, told me stuff about a baby named Julia, told me that she was with my uncle Eli, the character in the golfing hat. Well, who was it, then? I ask you. Who was it if *not* my mom?

This I learned: If my mother was relentless in her quest for me to be perfect ("Would a *stranger* tell you you look fat?"), it was because she loved me deeply. If she helped me too much and strangled my self-confidence, it was because, in her obsessive need to protect me, she literally could not stop herself from "paving the way." (She once convened a group of my elementary school colleagues at my home, fed everyone pounds of Mallomar cookies—and then talked the group into electing me Most Attractive Girl in 8B4. I still cringe at the memory.)

This I *definitely* learned: It is time to stop looking for my mom and for the mothers I wish both she and I could have been. It is time to start trusting another mother, even a larger mother than Jane—Mother Nature, mother spirit.

Did I learn all this from astrologers, psychics, parapsychologists, oracles? Somewhere in there.

One thing my mom and I always knew—even before her

death: We were inseparably connected—to each other and to my children and to their children and to her parents and to life before and life after. And we're still connected.

There's still a place where we meet on common ground, my mom and I. I love her. She loves me. Present tense.

In the mail this morning has come a review copy of *Best Loved Chinese Proverbs* by Theodora Lau. Everyone knows how wise the ancient seers were. Relying on synchronicity, can I open this little book and, blindfolded, point to three proverbs that will be appropriate to end my book—proverbs that will send messages to me and not to "To Whom It May Concern"?

Here goes. I close my eyes and open the book and point to where it says:

Do not be a frog sitting at the bottom of the well.   Yes! I will no longer have a limited view of life's possibilities!

Wheat stalks heavy with grain learn how to bow their heads. Bingo. Now that I no longer have a limited view, I have to try not to be as arrogant about my newfound open-mindedness as I was about my skepticism.

One who is as disappointing as an empty dumpling.   The good-looking, cerebral type who nevertheless told me last week that I was barking up a "loony tree" with this book?

And one more for good luck:

May a happy star always light your path.   Oh yes.

Resources

Spotlight!

DON'T GO INTO THE WORLD of the paranormal without a spotlight.

You need to cast light onto the believability factor. If I've learned anything from my adventures, it's this: There are good guys and there are bad guys in the game. It's so in every business from auto mechanics to orthopedics. It's certainly so in the business of the paranormal, where much is inexplicable and has to be accepted because intuition says it's so.

Like doctors, nurses, or auto mechanics, paranormal practitioners also can be careless and shoddy workers. Worse, many are outright phonies who deliberately fool their customers for cash and power rewards. These bad guys *need* a spotlight shining down on them. So do be skeptical. Frankly, an inquiring skepticism should *always* prevail, especially when dealing with the unprovable—and that goes for believers as well as nonbelievers. No one should look upon a paranormal practitioner with awe; no one wants to be taken in by the "Barnum effect"—named for the legendary circus showman who said, "There's a sucker born every minute." No one likes to be sucker punched.

Then again, if you're *only* skeptical, no new ideas can get through. You're in danger of turning into a crochety, dull-witted guest at the party of life. So don't look for easy excuses to dismiss what can't be measured by science. Be something in between gullible and skeptical: be open-minded.

Admit it: haven't you always been curious to see what would happen if you went to a psychic? Indulge that healthy curiosity. If I have any advice at all, it's this: *Give your experience a chance.* Sure, shine that spotlight on your paranormal encounters to see if they're valid for you—but don't use it just to find fault with the unprovable. Go for a balanced approach.

Here's the real rub: It's harder to shine a spotlight of truth on a psychic than on a doctor or an auto mechanic. There is no venue for a complaint about a prediction of passion that didn't materialize. The AMA doesn't want to know that your natal chart said your broken heart would heal—and it didn't. The Better Business Bureau doesn't want to hear that the oracle predicted you'd be promoted—and you weren't.

Still, you can protect yourself. There are ways to see through a psychic scam, guard against carelessness, root out charlatans. There are ways to find the good guys and ways to spot the phonies.

FINDING THE GOOD GUYS

How do you know when you're in the presence of a good spiritual practitioner?

First, it should be clear that the practitioner recognizes she or he has a supernatural gift and a spiritual connection, honors the place the gift comes from, and has the same honor and respect for the client. Further, the practitioner has the intelligence to guide others and transmit information in a way that's helpful, insightful, and often inspiring.

Sonia Choquette, author of *The Psychic Pathway,* is a well-known Chicago psychic, and she has some refreshing thoughts on the subject.

"Spiritual practitioners are not saints; they're merely FM radios as opposed to AM radios," says Choquette. "They're seven cylinders in a five-cylinder world, with abilities to perceive a broader range of vibrational patterns than those who have an undeveloped consciousness."

But how can the client be *sure* a practitioner really is a *sensitive,* really has the gift? "We all have 'organic knowing,' " answers Choquette. "You know. Trust your natural response. If you are made to feel self-conscious about who you are or incapable of your own creative problem solving, you're with an undeveloped practitioner. Note I said un*developed*—not inexperienced. You can have a thousand years of experience doing the wrong thing. A developed practitioner is always in a process of learning and growth—just as the client should be."

My own mom used to say, "I need the head of the department," when she was looking for the most expert worker—whether she was looking for a brain surgeon, a seamstress, or a baby nurse. She meant that she wanted the practitioner who'd made a mark at the top, who everyone knew was top-notch. And the way she found the head of the department? She asked around and finally called the one *most highly recommended by the most people.* Word of mouth.

You will not get good advice from a practitioner you've found through an ad or behind a gaudy storefront display. You shouldn't look for a brain surgeon *or* a great psychic through an 800 number.

Choquette says that "good practitioners get their clients by the process of attraction, not promotion—their work speaks for them." So the best way to find the "head of the department" is to ask people whose judgment you trust. Network. Also, ask around in *several* New Age bookstores; if the same name keeps turning up, it may be worth a shot. Or choose a name from the "Resources" section of this book. Many have found the listed practitioners to be excellent and have highly recommended their services. Maybe they'll be right for you.

Great practitioners seem to be *generally* wise and thoughtful people—and not just in their own fields, although admittedly that's my own subjective observation. Rick Jarow, the astrologist, could have been a professor in many genres (I later found out he was—at a prestigious eastern college). Leslie Austin, the past-life regression counselor, was a virtual font of information. This is not to imply that good practitioners must be sophisticated or have advanced university degrees; it *is* to imply that they are tuned in to the world around them. They are real people; you'd probably feel comfortable with them at dinner.

Cream-of-the-crop practitioners believe in what they do, and that brings a certain passion to their craft. "Somebody's boring me," said Dylan Thomas. "I think it's me." I personally think excellent practitioners should not be boring, and somehow, if they're playing a con game, if they're not invested in their work, they usually end up boring one to death with glittering generalities; that's because they're so jaded, they bore themselves.

Good practitioners, says Sonia Choquette, "are never absolute—'This is it and that's it.' They know that they can misinterpret. Good practitioners have a philosophical point of view: bad news is always perceived as an opportunity for growth. The first element a good practitioner will introduce at such news is gentleness, because growth is very painful."

Good practitioners, say satisfied clients, should help you to have insights about yourself in much the same way good psychoanalysts do: they should focus on your future and how you're go-

ing to live your life. Many are uncannily skilled as natural therapists who are able to offer injections of understanding, ways to or-
ganize a disorganized existence, and an intangible and comforting
sense of spirituality. Somehow we leave the good practitioner better able to interpret our lives and our loves. We feel comforted.
Wiser. More in control. We've gotten hope, reassurance—and,
not insignificant, the chance to talk.

How much should a good practitioner charge? Some say if the
person is truly spiritual, there would be no charge at all. "Nonsense," says Choquette. "We live in the Western world, not in India. The expectations you have of a spiritual worker and the value
you receive should be commensurate with the fee charged. Do
you place the same value on spiritual work that you would on a
good pair of shoes?"

Practically, fees do vary, as do those of doctors and lawyers, but
expect to pay anywhere from $50 to $300 for a reading. Establish
the fee before the consultation.

You can recognize good practitioners by the way they handle
difficult news. A practitioner, say experts, has a responsibility not
to upset a client. Some psychics, for example, operate in a trancelike state and don't mentally edit the material received: whatever
is seen, is reported. That operating style gave my friend Audrey a
stomachache. A psychic told her that her beloved dead husband
was angry at dying young, had not been ready to leave this life,
had a still-restless spirit. The psychic also told Audrey that in a
past life she'd been cruelly tortured to death. My friend came
away devastated.

When I told past-life practitioner Leslie Austin this story, she
commented, "The medium was in a trance and didn't know what
he was saying? Don't give me that bull. Part of him knew what he
was saying: a practitioner should never give up control. Anyone in
this business has a moral and ethical responsibility to be held ac-

countable for the transfer of information during a trance. True trances would never obscure responsibility. No wonder your friend's stomach hurt: she got kicked in the gut."

So it seems that good practitioners never terrify people with news of pending illness, death, or disaster. They want to help more than to be right.

"I don't proclaim doom and gloom, just as I don't solve other people's problems," says psychic Sonia Choquette. "While I won't withhold what I feel a client should know, I give the news with great restraint and gentleness. Actually, I see myself as Big Eunice at the switchboard, connecting people to where they need to go. A really good practitioner is a bridge. 'You need some real protection and support here—find a good attorney' or 'Your body seems out of whack—see a good doctor.' "

A parapsychologist says, "There are certain ethical issues here, involving self-fulfilling prophecies. Many easily influenced clients have been known to take dire predictions and actually make them happen—so great was their belief in the practitioner. A good practitioner simply won't make dire predictions."

There's one more important point: If spiritual practitioners have a responsibility to give readings of integrity, skill, and sensitivity, those who come seeking insights also have responsibilities.

"Spiritual practitioners work with their clients' vibrational energies," says Choquette, "and if your focus of energy is arrogant or manipulative, your reading will be faulty. A practitioner can only read what you've set up," she continues, "and if you come with *attitude,* if you approach with distrust and suspicion, if you take no responsibility for the quality of your own life, if you expect a magic show—your reading will fail."

Choquette thinks that clients obsessively bent on finding the holes in a spiritual practitioner's approach and focused on "getting" the practitioner instead of getting a good reading are bound for failure:

"Seekers have a responsibility to come with open hearts and be willing to examine parts of themselves that may not be comfortable; they must also be ready to look at their lives from a different point of view and they must try to be more creative in their solutions. In essence, they have to do their own work.

"Listen," says Choquette, "the only time a psychic can take advantage of you is when you go thinking someone else will do your work. And that's where the poop pile starts. If a client comes to me with the perspective that his life should get better after a conversation with me—and it doesn't, have *I* failed? Where is the client's responsibility? Has he exercised HIS choices? Has he come to me in good faith? Has he en*lightened* himself on what to expect? If you want a good reading—start *doing* some reading: learn about approaching a session with balance and fairness. Don't love that hoodoo-voodoo drama most people expect from us.

"For example," remembers Choquette, "a client came to me having spent a large money inheritance; she also had a husband who, with her knowledge, was having affair after affair. 'How can I make him love me again?' the client asked. 'How can I get my money back?' "

" 'I don't know,' I answered, 'since you're very committed to being a victim. You need to take responsibility for your own decisions.'

"Well, that client called me cruel and insensitive," says Choquette. "It made me sad—but, you know what—I wasn't cruel and insensitive. She expected her session would buy her the outcome she wanted and when it didn't deliver she was furious. My function is not to provide a free lunch: people who get duped are always the victims of their own desires for a free lunch."

Bottom line? A spiritual reading is a cooperative practice. You get as richly as you give.

SPOTTING THE PHONIES

Okay: you've set up a session with a paranormal practitioner. You're going to *try* to put aside your prejudices, try to see through different eyes, try to feel new things and think new thoughts. You understand that putting aside prejudices doesn't mean adopting dummydom.

You're also going to be fair and not write off the whole experience if a practitioner makes a few mistakes. Any psychic worth her intuition will always acknowledge the possibility of error: she may be influenced by your own intensity and pick up wrong vibes. She may have the chronology a little off or one part wrong and much of the rest correct; in itself, error does not mean a fraudulent or insensitive practitioner.

You won't *automatically* discard any portrait that doesn't match your own picture of yourself. We all wear armor to camouflage vulnerabilities; perhaps the practitioner has hit on a true aspect of you that needs acknowledging.

So, with that in mind, how would you actually spot a phony? Just what would the truth-telling glare of the spotlight reveal if you're in the presence of a scam artist? Well, a survey of paranormal practitioners, their clients, and the people who write about such things produced some warnings.

In order to avoid unscrupulous practitioners, it's the *best* idea to be tuned in to dubious catch phrases and shady practices. If you run into any of the following, find another practitioner.

I'll Just Light This Candle. Does the practitioner insist upon lots of heavy-duty showmanship that may include spooky rituals or symbols like candles flickering in the dark? Crystal balls? Arcane mumbled prayers?

It may be innocent—but more likely the show's an unskilled person's ploy to impress.

I Need More Money. Does the practitioner ask for a sum of money greater than the one agreed upon beforehand? If you're told to give up a sum to be blessed (and kept by the practitioner) or if you're told that an extra hundred dollars will make your lover come back—run, don't walk. You should always know in advance how much *in total* a session will cost.

I'll Erase the Curse. Does the practitioner make suggestions that only she or he can help you get rid of trouble/curses/bad karma? Again, run. One medium told a client that he had a cursed Toyota and he could get rid of the curse by lending it to the medium for a month. A responsible medium does not encourage dependency: just the opposite. One psychic told a client, "Give me two thousand dollars: I'll wear it taped to my body, which will make your husband come back." The client gave her the money, the husband didn't come back. Neither did the money.

What's That Book You're Reading? Many practitioners are pros at body language and nonverbal cues. Even if you think you've got a poker face, your eyes may widen or your mouth may tighten at a particular statement—and those are clues for the scam practitioner *and* a reason for him to expand on that particular subject. So if you notice the practitioner studying you a tad too carefully as he talks, think about what you're unconsciously giving away. A skilled reader can hit on what's bothering you simply by watching your reactions during his initial stock spiel—and feed back the information in such a way that you'll be amazed at how much he "knows" about you.

The manner of speech, choice of grammar, and eye contact of a client provide marvelous clues for a practitioner who relies more on observation than paranormal abilities. Clever readers can give you feedback about yourself that they obtain from visual—not paranormal—clues. The style, neatness, age, and cost of clothing or jewelry give a wealth of cues about a wearer's finances. For example, a *very* expensively dressed client may be shocked that a psychic "intuits" her husband may be a workaholic and pays little attention to her. A client carrying a book entitled *Stop Being a Victim* is reduced to tears when the reader "intuits" that she feels put upon from every direction. Dress blandly for an appointment to give the fewest clues possible.

What's on Your Mind? Psychic frauds have many techniques to get a client to offer clues to information they may then recycle back to him or her. If a practitioner asks you right off the bat, "What would you like to know about?" or "What's on your mind today?" perhaps she's looking for disclosures you don't know you're making. If, for example, you answer, "I want to know more about my relationship with my mother," it doesn't take a brain surgeon to guess that the two of you are having some problems; it's an easy segue from there to giving cliché advice on how people need *distance* from parents—advice that may seem right on the button and amazingly wise in your sensitive state.

Does What I've Said Make Sense? Readers often ask for feedback to know whether they should continue on the same track. Even if the reader has offered what you think is an extraordinary insight, don't fall down in amazement. While it's only fair to encourage a truly sensitive reader, reserve lengthy feedback (that may give information) till the reading is complete. Because most people, deep inside, want the psychic to succeed, and because most want to avoid discord—people tend to confirm even wishy-washy statements.

Goin' fishing is another way to ask for feedback. The practitioner "fishes," using questions as hooks: "Do you feel the presence of your dead mother?" If you answer no, he baits another hook with another subject. But if you answer yes, he reels in the fish (you) by turning the question into a statement. "Your mother *is* here, and that's why you feel her presence. She wants you to know . . ." Blah, blah, blah . . .

Send Me Your Life Story. Does the reader ask for information before you meet? Except in the case of an astrologer who definitely needs, in advance, your date, time, and place of birth so a complete astrological chart can be drawn up in readiness for your reading, most other practitioners should request nothing. For example, if you're told to provide photographs, business cards, or questions *in advance of* the meeting—be careful. It's one way unscrupulous seers get information.

Mr. Tall, Dark, and Handsome (or Maybe Mr. Short, Blond, and Plain Looking) Is Heading Your Way. The willingness of even sophisticated people to accept ambiguous, vague, or flattering statements is mind-boggling. Beware of glittering generalities. Almost everybody shares basic needs and fears, and general predictions or statements in these areas will often be considered amazingly correct by a client. Test it. How many of the following statements *could* be true for you?

- You need more love and support than most other people.
- You're trying to find yourself at this point in time.
- You feel guilty you're not doing enough for your family.

- The spirits say you've been deeply hurt by a trusted person.
- No one knows the real you.
- You're a very sensitive, intelligent human being.
- There's someone in your daily life who is your enemy.

You needn't be surprised if at least four or five or maybe all of the above statements apply to you: most people are still trying to find themselves, feel that they're sensitive, not really understood, need more love and support, etc., etc.

I'm Never Wrong. Yes, you are. Anyone who claims infallibility is not to be trusted. Ever.

I'm Licensed. No, you're not. Almost all mediums, psychics, and astrologers, for example, are self-ordained. There is no such thing (yet) as a controlled test to license a paranormal practitioner—which is not to say that gifted, consistently reliable sensitives don't exist.

Parapsychologists, on the other hand, although also not licensed as such, are generally scholars with advanced degrees. They're laboratory-trained scientists searching for evidence of psi phenomena under rigid scientific controls.

Please Don't Tape This. Although it's possible that a tape recorder may upset an honest paranormal practitioner (although I can't imagine why), most will allow you to tape-record a session. It's important to do so. First of all, people tend to place greater value on and remember correct statements more than they do wrong calls, so a poor reading, thought about hours later, can be recalled as a work of genius on the practitioner's part mainly because she mentioned your long-lost love's name—even though she made nine other ridiculous miscalls. Second, we do tend to forget things and listen selectively. It's enormously useful to replay a session to consider it in the entire context; you may see connections you missed during the drama of the actual experience. Third, we tend to emphasize the practitioner's place in the session and forget our own contributions. It's possible that you've casually dropped the name of your great-grandmother from France, immediately forgotten it—then forty-five minutes later the practitioner knocks you over by saying she has a message from a deceased person named Marie-Thérèse who has a Gallic accent. Thus, carefully reconsider anyone who refuses to allow the recording of a session where you can check all this.

Oh, That's What I Meant! Most statements can be interpreted many ways. Tell a clever scam practitioner that he's wrong when he says you had an abortion—it was a miscarriage—and he'll turn it around to "I *meant* you lost a baby, it wasn't clear *how.*" Be aware of grossly wide interpretations.

You Need Me. Beware of any practitioner who, overtly or even subtly, tries to create a psychological dependence. It's not terrific to be dependent on your mother, your child—*or* your psychic. "It's the responsibility of all professionals," says psychic Mary T. Browne, "to see to it that people don't become dependent on them. Therefore, 'I need to see you every day for the next month' should set up an immediate warning flag."

Sonia Choquette notes that "if the practitioner overestimates her own realm of influence, she becomes manipulative—and that's terrible. A *soulworker,*" says Choquette, "will help you think creatively—not in a linear fashion—about how to adjust your own life. A good psychic never solicits dependency. In my own practice, I see people no more than once a year."

Summing it up neatly, astrologer Rick Jarow says, "I don't believe that anybody should ever give up power to another person—

whether it's a doctor, counselor, astrologer, or psychic. Many ir-reputable people in this field will look for those willing to give up autonomy because they're basically insecure and want someone to tell them what to do. Use a psychic or an astrologer as you would a doctor or lawyer or any good consultant. These consultants may have information that can help you, but their word should never be taken as gospel."

Listen to What I Tell You—Not to Your Feelings. Wrong. Intuition counts. If someone seems like a sensible person, if the "vibes" are right in her presence, go with it. If every instinct tells you that your reading or experience is faulty—it probably is.

Well, If It's Not True Now, It Will Be True. This is one of the most common ploys to get out of a wrong call. Use your common sense here and ask for parameters like "During what time frame will it come to be true?" If the reader gives you a too broad response, like "Within the year," you can probably write off that call. You'll for-get to watch for the happening, unless it comes with high drama! Even more interesting is this: Often the practitioner *is* correct—not because of some greater intelligence to which she's privy, but because many people are so suggestible, they eventually make the things they hear come true. Charlatans know this, and when the client tells them they're wrong—they often compensate by saying the above. Be careful you don't use a reading to create a self-fulfilling prophecy.

For This Séance, It's Necessary to Keep the Room Dark and Our Hands Linked. Read this line as "I want you all to hold hands in my dark room so you can't reach out or see my secret apparatus and accomplices."

I Know All about You. Finally, several laboratory studies have shown that even an unskilled, untalented reader has excellent results in convincing a client that he knows her intimately by giving a *stock spiel he uses with every client.* The spiel is amazingly clever, but also amazingly, deceptively general. Most of us are sociable sometimes, reserved at others. Most of us like restrictions, are self-critical, and feel we have unused capacity. It sounds richly layered, but after reading the following stock spiel used by several popular psychics, you'll see that what they say could be true of almost everybody in the world. The stock phrase doesn't specify even one truly unique characteristic: check it out:

Some of your aspirations tend to be pretty unrealistic. At times you are extroverted, affable, sociable, while at other times you are introverted, wary, and reserved. You have found it unwise to be too frank in revealing yourself to others. You pride yourself on being an independent thinker and do not accept others' opinions without satisfactory proof. You prefer a certain amount of change and variety and become dissatisfied when hemmed in by restrictions. . . . Disciplined and controlled on the outside, you tend to be worried and insecure inside.

Your sexual adjustment has presented some problems for you. While you have some personality weaknesses, you are generally able to compensate for them. You have a great deal of unused capacity, which you have not turned to your advantage. You have a tendency to be critical of yourself. You have a strong need for other people to like you and for them to admire you.

Does it sound like you? Funny, I thought it sounded like me. And that's the problem.

Let the buyer beware.

PRACTITIONERS

In perusing the lists that follow, keep in mind that many practitioners, authors, or groups operate from a specific point of view: the Committee for the Scientific Investigation of Claims of the Paranormal, for example, will generally be critical of the paranormal. An organization formed to positively advance the concept of dowsing will do just that. A channeler who spends her life practicing and defending her discipline is not usually a paragon of open-mindedness.

But so what? Turn on your spotlight and venture out. You have nothing to lose and possibly other worlds to gain.

It is impossible to guarantee anyone's skill or integrity but each of the paranormal practitioners in this section has been highly recommended by at least two or more people.

I wish you luck in your journey.

Astrologers

Julian Armistead
212 369 8767

Lenore Cantor
212 243 2545

Susie Cox
520 326 2247

Arch Crawford
(Business Astrologer)
212 744 6973

James Greenleaf
360 354 1931

Rick Jarow
212 685 2848
914 485 2614

Michael Lutin
212 864 7447

Demo Di Mateli
212 533 4632

Bob Mulligan
P.O. Box 9237,
Naples, Fla. 33941
813 261 2840
(travels cross-country to do
readings)

Sioux Rose
(works in Spanish and English)
352 335 3827

Barbara Schermer
312 248 7108

Leda Serey
914 255 4435

Joanna Shannon
212 369 2585

Joan Smith
303 394 3056

Judy Turner
201 224 6629

Shelley Von Strunckel
212 787 6085
(In London) 011 4471 305961

Henry Weingarten
(financial astrologer)
212 661 9299

Smitty Wermuth
707 942 9154

Channelers

Andrew Bayuk
203 878 1833

Ann Blanchard
802 623 8111

Claudia Cusson
802 434 3479

Layla Oakland
802 728 4180

Kevin Ryerson
415 454 9727

Marcia Starck
505 473 1464

Cathryn Weser
505 466 1071

Dowsers

For a complete list of chapters (and recommendations for practitioners) call the American Society of Dowsers: 802 684 3417; fax 802 684 2565

Anne Williams
212 673 9257

Ron Warmouth
213 389 3483

Mediums

Rosemary Altea
The Croft
New Road
Woriaby Brigg
South Humberside,
England
DN2O OPE
011 441 652 618 229

George Anderson
516 586 0100 or
516 872 5325

Marisa Anderson
914 725 8871

Kathleen Karter
212 663 7434

Jane Grace Kennedy
212 595 2491

Patricia Mischell
513 563 1744 or
613 563 2427

Melvin Morse
212 572 2820

Alexander Murray
212 724 0934

Lita Rogers
404 874 7499

Tom Trotta
516 674 9836

Numerologists

Lloyd Cope
212 249 3144

Ken Nelson
414 242 1889 or
414 242 3857

Sioux Rose
352 335 3827

Frank Sígnorella
212 222 4454

Carol van Dermeir
212 777 1453

Parapsychologists

Contact the Rhine Institute for Parapsychology in Durham, N.C. (919 688 8241), or the Princeton Engineering Anomalies Research Laboratory in Princeton, N.J. (609 258 5950), if you're interested in participating in ESP research or if you wish information about the field of parapsychology.

Past-Life Regression

For a list of past-life regression therapists in your area, call the Association for Past Life Research and Therapies (909 784 1570).

Here are some recommended practitioners.

Leslie Austin, Ph.D.
212 460 9177

Denise Breton/Chris Largent
302 571 9570

Margaret Haas, M.A.
212 807 1286

Daniel Hutt
516 368 5105

Patricia Maguire, M.D.
201 567 4246

Barbara Pisick
212 734 9792

Judith Stanton, M.D.
716 275 4270

Brian Weiss, M.D.
305 661 6610
Fax 305 661 5311

Psychics

Rosemary Altea
The Croft
New Road
Woriaby Brigg
South Humberside, England
DN2O OPE
011 441 652 618 229

Marisa Anderson
914 725 8871

Dannion Brinkley
Fax 803 648 7271

Mary T. Browne
212 242 6080

Cattel
702 798 8448

Sonia Choquette
312 989 4744

Pat Craig
404 532 1251

Ellie Crystal
718 833 4264

Paula Deitch
818 501 0269

Joseph de Louise
312 332 1841

Marion Dyone Hensley
817 265 4002

Joy Herald
(specializes in finding lost people)
201 652 1177

Judy Hoffman
212 387 0701 or
212 534 6279

Hans Holzer
(specializes in ghosts)
212 580 9530

Irene Hughes
312 467 1140

Elizabeth Joyce
201 934 8986

Kathleen Karter
212 663 7434

Yolana Lassow
212 308 0836

Singh Modi
212 874 6169

Maria Moreno
818 919 6126

Maria Papapetros
212 935 4441

Beatrice Rich
212 988 4750

Tom Trotta
516 674 9836

Judy Turner
201 224 6629

Madame Betty Wells
301 739 2840

Joyce Winner
918 744 9411

For Information About a Psychomanteum

Dianne Arcangel
713 487 2131

Raymond Moody
205 835 2365

Tarot Readers

Frank Andrews
212 226 2194

Rosanna Rogers
216 751 1651

Peg Buckley
914 666 3543

Helen Satz
718 523 7009

Risa Cronin
407 265 2880

Cassandra Saulter
212 929 3490

Theresa Dratler
212 249 6999

Johanna Sherman
310 657 5590

Rosemary Gant
212 874 6493

Chuck Wagner
212 725 8849

Anni Pignatelli
213 391 3900

BOOKS

Althea, Rosemary. *The Eagle and the Rose*. Warner Books, 1995.

Anderson, George. *We Don't Die*. Berkley, 1989.

Auerbach, Lloyd. *Reincarnation, Channeling and Possession: A Parapsychologist's Handbook*. Warner Books, 1993.

Balcombe, Betty. *Everyone's Guide for Using Psychic Ability*. Samuel Weiser, 1996.

Bolen, Jean Shinoda, M.D. *The Tao of Psychology: Synchronicity and the Self*. HarperCollins, 1979.

Braude, Stephen E. *The Limits of Influence: Psychokinesis and the Philosophy of Science*. Routledge, Chapman and Hall, 1991.

Browne, Mary T. *Life after Death*. Fawcett, 1994.

Brinkley, Dannion. *Saved by the Light.* Villard, 1994.

Broughton, Richard S. *Parapsychology: The Controversial Science.* Ballantine, 1991.

Cayce, Edgar. *Edgar Cayce on ESP* (order from 1 800 711 9497).

Chopra, Deepak. *Ageless Body, Timeless Mind.* Harmony, 1993.

———. *The Way of the Wizard.* Harmony, 1996.

———. *The Path to Love.* Harmony, 1997.

Choquette, Sonia. *The Psychic Pathway.* Crown, 1995.

———. *Your Heart's Desire.* Crown, 1997.

Collins, Patricia. *Psychic New York.* City and Co., 1996.

Cox, Susie. *International Directory of Astrologers* (order from 520 326 2247).

Geller Uri. *My Story.* Praeger, 1975.

———. *The Geller Effect.* Henry Holt & Co., 1986.

Guiley, Rosemary Ellen. *Harper's Encyclopedia of Mystical and Paranormal Experience.* Harper/San Francisco, 1992.

Hastings, Arthur. *With the Tongues of Men and Angels: A Study of Channeling.* Harcourt Brace, 1991 (order from Institute of Noetic Sciences: 415 493 4430).

Hollander, P. Scott. *Tarot for Beginners.* Llewellyn Publications, 1995.

Holzer, Hans. *The Directory of Psychics.* Contemporary, 1995.

Jahn, Robert, and Brenda Dunne. *Margins of Reality.* Harcourt Brace, 1987.

Jussek, Eugene G., M.D. *Reaching for the Oversoul.* Nicholas-Hays, 1996.

Keen, Sam. *Hymns to an Unknown God.* Bantam, 1994.

Lau, Theodora. *Best Loved Chinese Proverbs.* HarperCollins, 1995.

LeShan, Lawrence. *The Medium, the Mystic and the Physicist.* Viking, 1966.

Lingerman, Hal A. *The Book of Numerology.* Samuel Weiser, 1994.

Llewellyn Books: P.O. Box 64383, St. Paul, Minn. 55164. (ask for catalog of books on mind and spirit)

Lyons, Arthur, and Marcello Truzzi. *The Blue Sense: Psychic Detectives and Crime.* Mysterious Press, 1991.

Moody, Raymond. *Reunions*. Villard, 1993.

Nadel, Laurie (with Haims/Stempson). *The Sixth Sense*. Avon Books, 1990.

Nickell, Joe. *Entities*. Prometheus Books, 1995.

———. *Secrets of the Supernatural: Investigating the World's Occult Mysteries*. Prometheus Books, 1991.

Riley, Jana. *Tarot Dictionary and Compendium*. Samuel Weiser Inc., 1995.

Roberts, Jane. *Seth Speaks*. Prentice-Hall, 1970.

Ross, T., and R. Right. *The Divining Mind*. Destiny Books, 1990.

Sagan, Carl. *The Demon-Haunted World*. Random House, 1996.

Schwartz, Tony. *What Really Matters*. Bantam, 1995.

Talbot, Michael. *The Holographic Universe*. HarperPerennial, 1991.

Tart, Charles T., Ph.D. *Open Mind, Discriminating Mind*. Harper & Row, 1989.

White, Suzanne. *Suzanne White's Guide to Love*. Harper/San Francisco, 1996.

Wiseman, Richard, Ph.D., and Robert Morris, Ph.D. *Guidelines for Testing Psychic Claimants*. Prometheus Books, (1 800 421 0351), 1995.

Wright, P. and D. *The Divining Heart* (The American Society of Dowsers Bookstore: 1 800 711 9497; can also purchase dowsing tools there).

Zukav, Gary. *The Seat of the Soul*. Fireside, 1989.

Periodicals

Common Boundary: P.O. Box 445, Mt. Morris, Ill. 61054-7819.

Exceptional Human Experience: Parapsychology Sources of Information Center, 2 Plane Tree Lane, Dix Hills, N.Y. 11746.

Gnosis: P.O. Box 14217, San Francisco, Calif. 94114-0217.

Journal of Parapsychology: 402 N. Buchanan Blvd., Durham, N.C. 27701-1728.

New Age Journal: P.O. Box 1988, Riverton, N.J. 08077-7588.

Noetic Sciences Bulletin; also *Intuition,* a journal: Institute of Noetic Sciences, 475 Gate Five Rd., Ste. 300, P.O. Box 909, Sausalito, Calif. 94966-0909.

Skeptical Inquirer: P.O. Box 664, Amherst, N.Y. 14226; 716 636 1425.

Tapes

Jungian Therapy (by Roger Woolger): 909 784 1570.
Life after Death. (Mary T. Browne): Simon & Schuster Audio.
Sounds True Audio: 1 800 333 9185.

ORGANIZATIONS AND FOUNDATIONS

- American Society for Psychical Research: 5 W. 73rd St., New York, N.Y. 10023; 212 799 5050.
- American Society of Dowsers Bookstore: Call toll-free for a catalog; 1 800 711 9497.
- Association for Past Life Research and Therapies: 909 784 1570.
- Association for Research and Enlightenment: 67th St. at Atlantic Ave., Virginia Beach, Va. 23451 (the son of famed Edgar Cayce, Dr. Charles Thomas Cayce, is president).
- Committee for Scientific Investigation of Claims of the Paranormal: P.O. Box 703, Amherst, N.Y. 14226; 716 636 1425.
- Common Boundary: P.O. Box 445, Mount Morris, Ill. 61054-7819 (wonderful conferences and journal).
- Institute of Noetic Sciences: 475 Gate Five Rd., Ste. 300, P.O. Box 909, Sausalito, Calif. 94966-0909; 800 383 1394 (supports research and education on consciousness and human potential; wonderful journal called *Intuition*).

- Institute of Parapsychology: 402 N. Buchanan Blvd., Durham, N.C.; 919 688 8241.
- Kairos Foundation: Chicago, Ill.; 312 329 0632.
- New York Open Center (courses in paranormal disciplines): 83 Spring St. New York, N.Y. 10012; 212 219 2527.
- Omega Institute (courses in paranormal disciplines): 800 944 1001.
- Parapsychology Foundation, Inc.: 228 E. 71st St., New York, N.Y. 10021; 212 628 1550.
- Parapsychology Sources of Information Center: 2 Plane Tree Lane, Dix Hills, N.Y. 11746.
- Princeton Engineering Anomalies Research Laboratory: School of Engineering/Applied Science, Princeton University, Princeton, N.J. 08544 (for experiments on ESP).
- Society for Psychical Research (SPR): 49 Marloes Rd., Kensington, London W8 6LA, England.

For further information on how to focus your spotlight or spot a scam, the following specialize in debunking paranormal activities.

- The Committee for the Scientific Investigation of Claims of the Paranormal: Paul Kurz, Chairman, P.O. Box 703, Amherst, N.Y. 14226-0703; 716 636 1425; fax 716 636 1733.
- Prometheus Books: 59 John Glenn Dr., Amherst, N.Y. 14228-2197; 716 691 0133.
- The Skeptic: P.O. Box 475, Manchester, M60 2TH, England.

AUTHOR'S NOTE

My search continues. If any reader wants to share an extraordinary, synchronistic, or otherworldly experience, possibly for inclusion in a new book or article, please write it out and mail it (along with the release on this page) to:

LAC
39th floor
295 Madison Avenue
New York, NY 10017

Release

The undersigned grants permission to Sherry Suib Cohen to publish the attached story in whole or in part in any medium.

Signature _____

Date _____

Index